THE CREATIVE DOER

the Creative Doer

A BRAVE WOMAN'S GUIDE FROM DREAMING TO DOING

By Anna Lovind

HAPPY ARTY PUBLISHING

a taste of what I can do
- a column
- a serialisation
- the odd article
travel a lot, drink a lot

For Jonna and Elsa,
who have made every single step
of this journey worth it.

Happy Arty Publishing
www.annalovind.com

Illustrations: Anna Lovind & Jonna Lovind
Graphic design: Lisa Zachrisson
Printed in Germany 2019
ISBN 978-91-519-1681-1

Contents

"Another world is not only possible, she is on her way.
On a quiet day, I can hear her breathing."

ARUNDHATI ROY

Why a woman's guide?

WHEN WE TALK about creativity we talk about universal truths, right? Yes, and no. The deep truths of creativity are universal. But the stories about the artist in our culture are not. They're stories about the male artist. The path of the lone genius, the starving artist, the irreverent rebel. All male. Not available to women, or only available at a great cost.

I want to talk about a different path. I want to take into account all the specific circumstances and challenges we face; not just because we are artists, but because we are female artists, living and working in a patriarchal world.

I believe gender is a sliding scale and that all of us find ourselves somewhere along it; sometimes in accordance with traditional conceptions about what it means to be male or female, sometimes contrary to those conceptions.

I'd love a world where it doesn't matter whether I'm a man or a woman, where the feminine and the masculine in me can blend in whatever proportions and I won't be labelled because of it. But that's not the case. From the moment we are born we are categorised as either or. Should we find ourselves somewhere in the middle, we are pushed – sometimes forced – to adjust. Should we find ourselves unable to adjust, we will find ourselves marginalised.

I believe that gender shouldn't matter, just as I believe race or class shouldn't matter, but we live in a world where it does matter. I've been raised a woman in a world where being a woman means doing and being certain things and not others. I've been raised in a world where men structurally hold the majority of power – politically, religiously, financially, militarily, as well as in the family.

This doesn't mean that all men hold actual positions of power, or that all women start on an equal footing. Cultural and societal power structures make up a complex web of intersecting identities and privileges. I can't assume that my experience is exactly the same as that of every woman. But what I can say is that regardless of our individual experiences as women, the qualities and traits we associate with the feminine are less valued than the qualities and traits we associate with the masculine. And since we have equated the feminine with woman, and the masculine with man, women are less valued than men.

To ignore this is to ignore my reality. If I wrote a book about the creative life without taking into account the circumstances and challenges that make my path different from that of my male peers, I would leave out the truth of my actual experience. I want to address those challenges and obstacles and I can't do that if I don't bring them into the conversation.

What are those challenges and circumstances? Well, where to start?

For women, it has been a long and arduous journey, even to be recognised as artists to begin with. It's a fairly recent thing for us to be allowed into the public creative arenas. In the 17th century, actors playing female parts were men dressed up as women, because women were not allowed on stage. Women painters were not admitted to art academies until the late 19th century. Women writers, well into the 20th century, used male pen names in order to have a shot at a fair reception. Some still do. The work of women artists and creatives has been universally overlooked for as long as patriarchy has been the governing structure of our world.

Sometimes this is the result of an intentional act; women's work is actually erased from the records. More often, it is the result of an unconscious filtering process. In a world so used to regarding the male perspective, the male voice, the male human as the norm, the filtering out of female voices and perspectives happens more or less automatically.

In 1929, Virginia Woolf gave us the story of Shakespeare's sister, as a response to the presumption that – since so few women geniuses have been recorded in history – women must simply lack the brilliance of men. Woolf wrote an unsentimental account of what would have happened to a girl of equal talent and passions, had she tried to pursue the path of the creative genius in Shakespeare's days. While this path led her brother to unparalleled success, for her it led to utter destruction, her life ending almost before it had a chance to begin.

Things have changed since Shakespeare's days, and since Woolf's days too. I'd love to say that everything has changed and the playing field is now even for men and women, but let me line up a few examples from the literary world to make it clear that's not the case.

In 1996, Bloomsbury Press asked Joanne Rowling to use only her initials on the cover of the first Harry Potter book, because they believed the book wouldn't appeal to boys and men if it had a female author's name on the spine.

In 2015, US writer Catherine Nichols conducted an experiment. She sent her manuscript out to agents under her real name, and then again under the male pseudonym George

Leyer, receiving drastically different responses. "Under my own name, the same letter and pages sent 50 times had netted me a total of two manuscript requests... George sent out 50 queries, and had his manuscript requested 17 times. He is eight and a half times better than me at writing the same book."

A study of more than two million titles published between 2002 and 2012 revealed that books written by women are priced at forty five per cent less than those penned by men.[1] Even when taking into account that women more often write for lower-priced genres (which is a whole other topic for discussion) a gap of nine per cent still remains.

Women consistently receive fewer prestigious awards, from the Nobel Prize to the Booker to the Pulitzer. In spite of decades of criticism and efforts to change this, male writers still claim on average two thirds of the American prizes. And it's not just that fewer women writers win; when it comes to female characters, the numbers are even worse. None of the protagonists in the last fifteen novels to win the Pulitzer Prize were women or girls. The literary world, it seems, doesn't like books by or about women.

This under-representation is not unique to the literary world. For every woman named in current Swedish history schoolbooks, on average eleven men are named. In the US, women are the focus of ten per cent of news stories, and comprise twenty per cent of experts or spokespeople interviewed. In the UK, one per cent of venture capital deals in 2017 went to businesses with female founders. Work by women artists makes up three to five per cent of major permanent collections in art museums in the US and Europe.

I could keep listing examples but I'd wear you out. The numbers are depressing. Most of them are improving steadily but slowly. Slower than I'd like. Slower than seems reasonable.

This way, the stories of women – as well as the women themselves – are excluded from the collective narrative. This matters.

Where I live, women are rarely refused education; we are allowed to manage our own money, we have the right to vote and decide whom we want to marry. The inequalities we face today are often more insidious.

The sexual objectification of women in the media landscape can hardly be called insidious. It's everywhere – in the beauty and fashion industry, in advertising, in movies, TV shows and magazines, on social media, in the gaming and the porn industry. The connection between the increasingly unachievable beauty standards created and perpetuated in these arenas, and young girls' lack of self-esteem, is fairly straightforward. So is the connection to increasing rates of eating disorders.

But the way it affects us as creative beings might be less obvious. Objectification leads to self-objectification – "a key process whereby girls learn to think of and treat their bodies as objects of others' desires", as described by Barbara L. Frederickson and Tomi-Ann Roberts.[2] From an early age, we learn to view ourselves from outside, always monitoring the way others see us, in order to present ourselves favourably and please the male gaze. According to Professor of Politics Caroline Heldman, women engage in this kind of monitoring on average every thirtieth second. This doesn't just consume a lot of energy and reduce available cognitive functioning in the brain; it also creates a split inside, a disconnection from our own experience in favour of the perceived experience of others.

The originality of our creative work is directly related to our ability to see the world from our own unique viewpoint and stay true to that viewpoint. In order to express our unique truth, we need to stand firmly rooted in our own selves and look at the world from the inside out. Women learn the exact opposite. We learn to internalize the perspective of the other, of an external (male) observer, and in doing so, our own perspective, and even reality, is lost.[3]

If the creative work we feel called to do challenges the known and accepted, we need self-esteem as well as self-confidence to take the risk and do this work publicly, because it leaves us vulnerable to other people's judgements. "Confidence is the stuff that turns thoughts into action", as psychology professor Richard Petty put it. Other factors play a part as well, but he has a point.

Women generally have lower self-esteem than men, and even less self-confidence,[4] not just when it comes to looks and body image, but professional abilities as well. As a rule, women consistently underestimate their abilities, whereas men overestimate theirs, even when in reality their actual performance does not differ in quality or quantity. Women are also less likely to take risks in their work life.

Why? Some suggest this female risk-aversion has roots in biology. Writer Tara Mohr offers a different explanation – school very effectively teaches girls to follow the rules. We do as we're told, follow the instructions, give the right answers; and in return we are rewarded with good grades and plenty of approval. The Good Girl is the winner of the current school system. Unfortunately, in work life, her strategy is no longer successful. If you always play by the rules, if you expect to be rewarded based on merit only and if you patiently await your turn rather than take the risk of promoting yourself, chances are that someone who was encouraged to be bold rather than obedient when he grew up, who maybe doesn't have the best grades but plays golf with one of the board members, and who isn't afraid to pitch his ideas without being asked to, is going to cut in front of you and claim the job.

Actually, "chances are" is a gross understatement. Men hold a staggering nienty four per cent of the chief executive positions in the US and numbers are similar in Europe.[5] There's a reason for this, and it has been proven time and again that the reason is not that men are better at what they do.

We don't need to become daredevils in order to live creative lives. We don't need to elbow our way into the arena and try to compete with men on their terms. In fact, let's not, because the system is not rigged in our favour.

> "Soon we realize that however hard we try to be good men, we are not judged the same way, paid in the same way, we have to work harder and longer to prove ourselves worthy, and even then we are still not enough."
>
> LUCY H PEARCE

But it's good to become aware of where our aversion to risk-taking is coming from. Because even if we have zero interest in making a career in the corporate world, these behavioural patterns matter. If you were raised a Good Girl, or learned to become one in school, this might be holding you back as a creative. Doing creative work means risking failure, breaking the rules sometimes, being misunderstood sometimes, being seen as weird, being met with disregard or disapproval – basically the Good Girl's worst nightmare.

Then there's motherhood – perhaps the biggest divider of all. Historically, if you chose to become a mother, you chose to end your creative career.

For a long time, I didn't realise that so many of the women

artists I admired didn't have kids. Like Virginia Woolf, Sark, Oprah, Natalie Goldberg, Ann Patchett, Gloria Steinem, Frida Kahlo, Helen Mirren, Dolly Parton, Elizabeth Gilbert, Selma Lagerlöf, Georgia O'Keeffe, Coco Chanel, Joni Mitchell (who gave her baby up), Arundhati Roy and Jane Austen.

I didn't even think about it until I had my first child and it struck me how ill-prepared I was – and how little I knew about how – to combine motherhood with a creative life. I looked at these brilliant women and the realisation that none of them had done it either was disheartening. What did it mean? Wasn't it possible? I started looking for women who had done what I was trying to do – combine a creative career with motherhood.

I found Sylvia Plath, and my heart sank as I read about her heroic but losing struggle to survive as an artist who also found herself a single mother of two young children. Everything about her story confirmed what was held as true at that time; that the conflict between a woman's artistry and her female identities (wife and mother) is too strong – even, potentially, deadly.

I read *The Red Shoes*, Rosemary Sullivan's biography of Margaret Atwood, whom I deeply admired, and found the same conflict described; a talented young woman trying to find a way in a culture that positions womanhood and artistry as antithetical, particularly a woman's family life and artistry.

Atwood, however, rejected this position and went on to prove it wrong. She had her marriage, her child *and* her career as a writer. She cautioned us though, saying that it was possible because she was able to support herself financially through her writing. Had she needed to add a second job to the mix, it wouldn't have worked, she said.

When I searched, I found many women artists who had

kids. Like Toni Morrison. Patti Smith, Audre Lorde, Alice Munro, Vanessa Bell, Maya Angelou, Joan Didion, Alice Walker, Tori Amos, Sigrid Hjertén and Meryl Streep, among many others.

Many of them did brilliantly. Some of them actually had the second job Atwood cautioned against and managed to make it work. Did they have to work harder? No doubt. Did they pay a price for wanting both? For sure.

There's a reason so many of the women artists we know don't have kids. We already face challenges and obstacles simply because we're female in a male-dominated arena. Having children complicates matters to such an extent that, depending on your individual circumstances, your financial situation, your support systems etc. it might simply become undoable.

Today we can get help. There's day care and baby-sitters and equal parenting, and we have a better chance of creating a structure that allows us time to devote to our craft than our sisters from a hundred years ago. And then the kid gets what feels like the tenth cold in a month and our neat structure is fucked. Because in an overwhelming majority of families, the mother still carries the main responsibility for the daily care of the children. She is the one who is expected to, and who will, stay at home, forsaking other ventures to tend to her littles. It is implicit in the question always asked of a professional woman: "How do you balance your work and family life?" According to our cultural script, it's still up to her to balance it.

It makes me think of a few lines in a book about creativity I read a couple of years ago, where the male author wrote about how nothing can stand between the artist and his work, if true commitment is there. As an example, he mentioned how Dostoevsky had twelve kids but didn't let that stop him from writing his books.

I didn't know whether to laugh or cry when I read that. "What about Dostoevsky's wife?", I wanted to ask. The woman who stayed behind caring for all the twelve kids so he could go off and write. How would she have gone about it, if she wanted to write?

I'm not saying she did. I'm just saying someone needs to care for the children. If the baby needs food or wakes up crying, even the muse will have to stand back.

Is it an option for a woman to discard her parental obligations in pursuit of her art? Men do it, have done it throughout history without anyone raising an eyebrow. What happens if a woman chooses to behave the same way?

Women are still socialised from an early age to please, to place the needs of others before their own and to derive their sense of value primarily from their relationships. Can someone raised like that choose the life of the artist if that choice means she neglects her children? Of course she can, but it'll cost her a lot more than it would a man, personally and professionally. It'll require her to go against upbringing and cultural expectations and others will judge her for it. Hard. She will judge herself too.

The male genius is often presented as reckless, utterly irresponsible about everything but his art. He's uncompromising, but in a way we can't help but admire a little. A male artist gets away with it. A female doesn't.

Just consider this quote from writer Henry Miller.

"From the little reading I had done I had observed that the men who were most in life, who were moulding life, who were life itself, ate little, slept little, owned little or nothing. They had no illusions about duty, or the perpetuation of their kith and

kin, or the preservation of the State. They were interested in truth and truth alone. They recognized
only one kind of activity ... creation."

It's pretty irresistible, isn't it? I know I've fallen for it, time
and time again. The fire he describes. The single-minded
determination. That's the Artist, as we know him. Disregard-
ing worldly troubles, delegating the care for kith and kin to
others. Because he can.

Very few women can or will make that choice, and honestly, why would we want to? As seductive as it sounds, it's
ultimately a path of self-absorption and recklessness.

What I'm interested in is what does devotion look like if
it doesn't mean forsaking everything and everyone, including
your kids, for art?

Margaret Atwood gave us one clue when she told us only
so many things fit onto our plates. I still haven't found all the
rest of the clues, but I've found a few, in the safe spaces we
create together, in the consistent and persistent doing of our
work, in the brave telling of our stories.

"Those who tell the stories rule the world."
HOPI PROVERB

For far too long, men have told all the stories. This is changing, but the male narrative is still the norm. Remember those
prize-winning novels where not a single one was told from
the perspective of a girl or woman? The assumption that man
equals human is still pervasive in media, art, politics and reli-
gion, and as Ursula K. Le Guin points out, it's related to a few
other assumptions, equally problematic: that we're all white;
that we're all straight; and that we're all of Christian assent.
These assumptions are usually made by privileged groups;

What I'm interested in is what does devotion look like if it doesn't mean forsaking everything and everyone, including your kids, for art?

less often by minorities who, in the words of Le Guin, "know all too clearly the difference between 'us' and 'them'".

It's time we tell our own stories. It's time we centre ourselves in the narrative of the creative life so that we can begin to incorporate the diversity of perspectives that is the truth of the human story.

When presented with the male view as the human view, we can then say, No, actually, this is what it looks like from where I stand. That's what happened in the fall of 2017, when #metoo swept across the world and stories in the millions poured from previously silent women about their experiences with sexism and sexual assault. Women rose collectively and claimed their perspectives to be valid and important – just as relevant for everyone to hear as the prevalent male perspective.

These stories opened eyes and started conversations. And now we need more. We need stories about the wrongs, the horrors and the abuse, and we also need stories of the everyday, the mundane, the small and seemingly insignificant. We need every aspect of the world explained and shown to us from a woman's point of view – or from women's points of view, rather, because it's not a single story. We need our articles, our novels, our photographs, our inventions, our paintings, our craft and our discoveries. We need the stories of our womanhood and sisterhood, our daughterhood and motherhood. All of it needs to be shared and told and heard, and consciously woven into the story of our human experience.

*"Darling, you feel heavy because you are too full of truth.
Open your mouth more. Let the truth exist somewhere
other than inside your body."*

DELLA HICKS-WILSON

Why I wrote this book

I WAS A sensitive, quiet child. An introverted watcher and
listener. As soon as I learned how to, I began to write down
what I saw and heard and experienced. In my first years of
school I wrote a lot of poetry, much of it dark and trouble-
some. I wrote poem after poem about mistreated animals
wasting away in some corner, covered in wounds that
wouldn't heal, their suffering strangely invisible to the people
around them.

My choice of topics raised a few eyebrows. I got a lot of
praise for the advanced use of language. Nothing more. But it
was all there; that little eight-year-old was writing it all, the
terror of being sexually abused, the pain of not being seen,
even though no one understood what she was trying to say.

Writing helped keep my head above the surface when our
family fell apart, when we lost our home and I was exposed
to more abuse by people who came and went in our lives.
All through my teens I filled journal after journal, trying to
channel the increasing pressure inside into something that
would make sense; that would keep me from hurting myself
or the people I loved. My words burned on the paper and for
a little while it burned less inside.

At that time, I never aimed to create something. Creativity was not a even a word in my vocabulary, I didn't think of myself as creative and no one else ever suggested I was; I just needed the writing in order to survive.

I look at her now, this beautiful young girl. Intelligent and wise beyond her years in a way that fooled every adult who came her way, that earned her top grades even though she barely attended school, that landed her huge responsibilities when she could not even take care of herself. All the words she could not say, the truths she could not express burning her from the inside out, burning increasingly brighter, like a supernova heading for her own destruction.

After an attempted suicide at eighteen, I was locked up in a psychiatric ward because I was considered a danger to myself. At that point I could no longer write.

It took me years to find my way back but eventually, I started creating again. I wrote songs, I diddled with the guitar, I discovered watercolours, I wrote articles, poetry and as always, journal after journal. And slowly, slowly, my creativity came to be something more than a survival skill. It came to be about expressing myself – and not just my pain, but all of me. It came to be about connection, once I felt safe enough to start sharing my work with others. And as my commitment deepened, my creative work became a vehicle for change – in myself and others.

I know now that in order to access my own voice and my true stories I need to be present for my own experience. I need to stay present to the experience of being a female, living in a world where being in a female body is not safe, where the female voice and perspective is not valued, and this is a scary thing to do. If I am to do it, safety is required. Safe spaces, safe practices.

I've learned that this is true not only for me, but for all

women. Women have been on the losing end of patriarchy for thousands of years, and all that talk of fearlessness is of zero use to us. If we are to go deep with our work, start sharing our truths and allow ourselves to be seen – safety is required.

To acknowledge this is not a matter of giving in to excuses, or playing small, or being a victim to circumstances. It's a matter of seeing what is and starting from there, instead of trying to walk in the boots of someone whose circumstances are radically different from mine.

This is still the road less travelled. That's why I'm writing this book, because I want to explore this road, this third path. Being a woman and an artist – particularly a professional artist – is a relatively new combination of roles to take on. Add motherhood to the mix and we're in uncharted territory. We are shaping the path as we go here. We are shaping the path for ourselves, for each other and for our artist daughters.

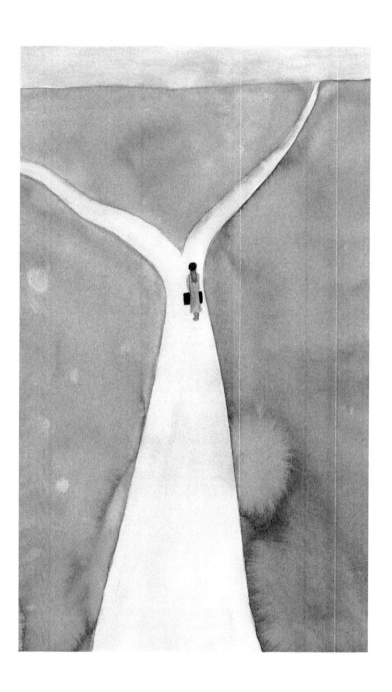

CHAPTER 1

What do you want?

"You too can be carved anew by the details of your devotions."
MARY OLIVER

BEFORE WE BEGIN, I want to clarify something. When I use the word "work" in this book I mean your creative work, whether it is your paid job or not.

The word "work" has gotten a bad rap, particularly in the self-help industry. I guess because of its associations to traditional career hustling and cubicle boredom. The soul draining employment that eats away at your time and your life. I get it.

Find your passion, we say instead. Go for joy, easy is right. And passion is good, joy is necessary, but it's still only part of it. Another part of the equation is work. Beautiful hard work. The deeply gratifying experience of using our hands and hearts and minds to make things happen, to move something from idea into form.

Calling it play instead doesn't sum it up. Play has its place. But so has inspired effort, the practical daily tending to a mission that is not always easy or playful. And it doesn't have to be easy to be meaningful and nourishing.

The fluffy language only serves to keep us naïve about what it means to do your heart's work. Easy is right, sure. The feeling of ease and flow is a great indicator that the direction we've chosen is right, but it's a state of grace and grace is a gift, not a given. This is a human journey. It involves both grace and hard work.

Our ideas and dreams come from somewhere beyond our human minds, that's for sure. The creative powers of this universe are greater than us, and what we can create when we partner with those creative powers exceeds anything we can manage on our own. But we're not simply vessels. We're co-creators and our work is required. Without it, even the most beautiful idea will not make it into form.

So, let's leave the unicorns in the stable for this ride, because although this is a journey towards joy and creative freedom, it's not necessarily an easy one.

Your path is your own

What do you want?

"The point of this question is to make sure your goals are your own – that they come from your heart, not from some idea about who you should be and what your life should look like.

They say that when you are about to get married, you need to plan for a marriage, not just a wedding. The same applies here. Whatever creative work you choose to devote yourself to, you are going to be spending a lot of time and energy on it. It will be your close companion for a long time. So make sure you truly want it, all of it, the actual work, the day-to-day doing, the LIVING of this creative dream; not just the potential rewards when you're done.

As women, we are encouraged to desire such strange things. Most of them have to do with looks, romance and approval. We are rarely encouraged to go deep with our desires, to find out how wildly powerful we truly are, and what the landscapes that truly fit our souls look like. So when asked the question "What do you want?", our answers often come from the surface level.

Those surface-level answers are based on what we have decided, often subconsciously, is possible for us. What we are allowed and expected to do, what our parents and partners and peers would approve of, what we've seen other women do, what the market wants, what would look good, or simply what feels safe.

What I want is for us to leave that aside for a bit. I want us to take a step back from the shoulds and the oughts and turn our attention towards our own deep desires. Because listening to and acting on our deep desires is how we create a life and work that actually feels like our own.

But it's not going to happen unless we give ourselves permission to choose what our hearts are asking us to choose.

This permission must be granted over and over again. We must educate ourselves on why we feel we don't have the right or the ability to go for what we truly want. Is this just our individual struggle, or is it something all women artists face? Is it the struggle of all women artists or something only coloured women artists, or queer women artists, face? And so on. Knowledge is power. Once we know what we're up against, we can take informed action.

For every choice you make, every wrong or right turn, it will become clearer and clearer what works for you. You will become more discerning when it comes to whose advice you listen to. You will learn that someone else's path is just that – someone else's path. It is what worked for them and their specific circumstances, at that specific time. And before you beat yourself up for not being as productive as the author of that book, you will find out if he too is a working parent of three who is weaving creative magic late at night when the kids are asleep, without the help of a team. If not, his advice might not be applicable to your life. You will give yourself permission to pick what's relevant to you and leave the rest. This sense of discernment is crucial.

Learn from those ahead of you, by all means, but make sure you have your compass securely fixed on your own true north.

Pain pushes until vision pulls

Some wise person said that pain pushes until vision pulls. The first time I heard those words they shook me to the core. Because in my work – even in my creative work – I had always been pushed and motivated by pain and fear; fear of not being perfect, of not making it, of not getting what I needed and wanted. I had been running all my life to get ahead, driven by the fear of what would happen if I didn't make it.

In a brief moment of insight, I felt how utterly exhausting it was and also what a bliss that other alternative would be – to be pulled forward by the power of my vision.

Instead of being pushed by fear to take action, I could connect with my dream and let the strength of that vision pull me towards it. Instead of grabbing and grasping, I could turn towards what I want and ask it to come create with me. I could rely not only on my own, limited power, but on the creative powers of this universe – the power of a vision that wants to be born into this world, and that seeks me to accomplish it.

I didn't fully understand how this co-creation works – I still don't – but I could instinctively sense the enormous power of it, and I also understood that in order to access that power the vision had to be true. Not some compromised, half-assed version of it. Not "I actually want to be a poet but no one reads poetry, so I'll become a journalist instead." No. Your true desire.

Over time, I've learned that the most powerful pull did not come from the vision I figured out myself, but from the one that just came to me once I learned to listen deeply.

This is key.

If you've spent most of your life NOT listening deeply to yourself, and many of us have, it will take some practice. You will not just sit down, close your eyes and hear a voice spill all the details about your true dreams. But maybe there will be a hunch, a hint, some curiosity, a sense of lightness in one particular direction. That's your answer for now.

So when I ask the question "What do you want?" I don't want your quick, surface answer. I want you to pass that question on to some deeper aspect of yourself and see what truths rise to the surface in response. Those truths will shape your roadmap.

How do you want it?

The next question is more practical, but equally important. How do you want it? What fits with your current life circumstances? What suits your temperament? What feels natural to you?

These are crucial questions, because you can be absolutely clear about the dream you want to see come true and still make a mess of it if you don't take into account what your actual day-to-day life looks like.

If you're a mother, for instance, you likely won't have

Over time, I've learned that the most powerful pull did not come from the vision I figured out myself, but from the one that just came to me once I learned to listen deeply.

hours and hours of uninterrupted time to do your work. Let go of the idea that you need it; it will only frustrate you. The "room of our own" you need in order to create might not be a cabin in the woods that you can disappear to and emerge six months later when your novel is done, it might be the kitchen table at night when the kids have fallen asleep, or the rare weekend at a friend's house. We create in the midst of life.

To make our dreams happen, nothing is asked of us that we can't give. We're not required to abandon ourselves, our needs or our relationships in order to make this happen. Our assignment here is simply to figure out how to incorporate our creative work into our lives in a way that works – that might even feed and nourish the rest of it.

To begin with, what would your creative life look like if it were completely up to you? Do you want to be able to do your thing full time, or just have enough free time to play around with what you love on a regular basis? Do you want to start a business to sell the stuff you make, or is your yearning simply to infuse your day-to-day life with a sense of beauty and creativity? Do you want to dedicate time to learning more in order to be able to practise the work you do on a new level?

What is it that you want?

Only when you allow yourself to follow your deep desires AND do it in a way that fits you and your life, will you find the sustainability you need to keep going, long-term. It's a lot of work, bringing a dream to life. You'll need all the fuel you can get and the best kind of fuel is your own love for what you do.

Redefine creative work

I believe it's important that women are allowed equal access to the professional arenas of creativity, as working artists. I think equal representation in literature, museums, committees, media, among awarded and recognised artists and so on is necessary. But I also think it's necessary that we broaden our view of creativity and look beyond those acknowledged arenas. The focus on being recognised and anointed by a few select institutions is part of the old, patriarchal view of artistry. It's an individualistic path, highly competitive, and it fosters a culture of superiority and grandiosity where the winners are geniuses, different from and better than the rest of us. And because of this high status, they can behave as they like. They are The Artists.

And when I say behave as they like, I don't just mean they get to be self-absorbed narcissists who are difficult to work with, I mean they literally get away with almost anything. To name just a few, consider William Burroughs, Norman Mailer, Charles Bukowski and Pablo Neruda, who have all admitted to abusing, raping or even murdering women. And they're still widely celebrated as geniuses – their crimes rarely even mentioned, or only mentioned in passing with a reference to drug abuse or mental illness.

That men like them are now beginning to be held accountable for their words and actions, regardless of their status as creative geniuses, is a fairly recent turn of events, courtesy of the global #metoo uprising. If it will affect the way we value and canonise the work of violent, misogynist men remains to be seen, but their armour has been severely dented and their halos are slipping. This is good news. As creatives, we really don't want to be following in their tracks anymore.

Essentially, the path of the Male Genius is about becoming great or nothing. Which means a whole lot of creative work gets dismissed as nothing.

What about the everyday expressions of creativity that we can neither quantify nor monetise? That's the creative arena traditionally inhabited by women. It might look like creating a home of beauty and comfort, finding always new ways to support the growth and development of children's mind and souls, creating gardens of play, beauty and nourishment, creating food, creating style, creating community. It's the thousand small acts of making our lives more beautiful and meaningful and the results of all this work are often perishable (we eat the food). It's not recognised as creative work, but it is nonetheless.

Making money is only one way of measuring the value of our creative work and it's not the most accurate one. Neither is fame.

Why do we value one and not the other?

For a long time, Karin Bergöö Larsson was known only as the wife of internationally-renowned painter Carl Larsson, and as the mother of his eight (!) children. But before they met, she was a promising young painter in her own right. In 1877 she was one of the very few women admitted to the Royal Academy of Arts in Stockholm. After completing her studies, she went to the artists' colony in Grez-sur-Loing, France, to continue painting. Then love struck. She met fellow painter Carl Larsson and within a year they were married and she was pregnant with their first child.

At that time, there wasn't much of a choice. She couldn't do both. She left painting for motherhood and managed to find new channels for her creativity within the bounds of home. Today she is recognised as one of the most influential interior designers of her time. Inspired by the Arts and Crafts movement, she modernised the dark and stuffy Victorian interiors of her time and created what later became known as the Swedish Style.

Was she content? Did she resent the fact that her husband got to continue his career as a painter while she couldn't? Did she resent his fame, when her own creative path rendered neither fame nor money? I'll never know. I look at her and see a lack of choices and the loss of a gifted painter. I also see incredible resilience; a creativity that refused to be held back, and that burst into being through whatever means available.

Can I regret the fact that she didn't get to pursue a professional career and still appreciate what she created in her life? I think so.

What I know for sure is that our everyday creativity is still not valued properly, by ourselves or in society at large. It's often not even recognised as creative work at all. But for most of us, the everyday is where we begin to experience and exercise our creative powers. This is where we get to learn what we enjoy and what we're good at. If we were to recognise the value of this – all the creative work we already do in our everyday lives – it would help prepare us. It would build our confidence as we stretch towards new arenas and new levels of creative work.

Don't be fooled by the language of greatness, genius and burning passion. The clues to the creative life of your dreams can usually be found in the everyday creativity you already engage in – the quiet, unassuming creative work that doesn't necessarily burn down the house, but holds the seeds to some magic only you can unfold.

You need to know what you want right now but you do not need to know where it will lead you. You do not need to know the end goal or how it will all fit together.

Let go of the One Big Purpose

Searching and waiting for that passion to flare up is actually a common reason for why we lack clarity about what we want. We're trying to find our One Big Purpose and we have to know what it is before we can act on it, right? So we wait and we search and we try to figure it out, and the clarity doesn't come.

The thing is, you need to know what you want right now but you do not need to know where it will lead you. You do not need to know the end goal or how it will all fit together.

A few of us will have what can be described as one big calling, where you've known since childhood that you will become a priest or that music is the only option. But for most of us that's not the case. Sometimes we can't hear our deep desires speak because they have been buried under layers and layers of conditioning, fear and other people's opinions. Sometimes we simply don't know what we want. We don't yet know the shape and form of our talents and dreams. There's just that longing, that urge inside.

Uncovering what we feel called to do is a step-by-step process. And we don't just get one shot. Our creative soul is always calling us, in different ways at different times in our life. Dream after dream will come knocking, wanting to be born. Our work will evolve and change as we do; it will be a winding journey and information will often be given on a need-to-know basis. All you need to know to get started is what is calling you right now. And when I say what is calling you, I simply mean what you are curious about; what feels joyous; what you feel like exploring; or what you want to express. What we're looking for is often simple and close to home.

Start before you're ready

A common way we keep ourselves from starting is waiting to feel ready. This could keep us waiting a very long time. In traditional work life, there might be a job description that lets us know if we've got the qualifications we need. When it comes to our creative work, there are no job descriptions and we are never fully qualified. In order for you to grow as a creative, you're asked to stretch beyond your comfort zone, over and over again. It's risky business.

Sometimes we're waiting for circumstances to be more favourable. We convince ourselves that as soon as we have more money, more time, more space, we'll get going. Mary, a gifted artist friend of mine, would always refer to her creative work as something that was soon about to start for real. She was just waiting for this or that to change first. One of the recurring themes was the lack of space in her home where she could do her work. When we move to a more spacious flat it'll be easer, she'd say. But they kept moving to bigger places and she kept repeating the same thing.

Finally, they moved to a big house where she would have all the space she needed to really go for it with her creative work. One day, about when their extensive renovations were done, we sat at her kitchen table and she showed me a couple of sketches she had made. The sketches showed a turret she wanted to build, attached to the south end of the house. "Imagine having my studio at the top of that tower," she said, stardust in her eyes. "It would be so much easier to work there," she continued. "It would be quiet, I wouldn't have to listen to the kids fussing, I could leave my stuff out and ..." She looked at me and her voice trailed off. We both burst into laughter. She had everything she needed in order to get to work, except for a turret? Really?

The thing is, you will never feel quite ready. Circumstances will never be perfect. You'll have to start anyway.

It might not sound like it, but this is fear speaking. As long as you postpone your dream, you don't have to risk failing. But failure is as integral to creative work as it is unwanted, and there is absolutely no way you can protect yourself from it. Failure is how we learn about our strengths and weaknesses; it's how we discover what works and what doesn't. If you understand what failure is for, you can use it to refine your skills and sharpen your aim. The Good Girl in you will do anything to avoid it, and in doing so, she will make sure your creative dream remains a dream.

The thing is, you will never feel quite ready. Circumstances will never be perfect. You'll have to start anyway.

To start before you're ready is to place yourself in unfamiliar territory, in a version of your life slightly bigger than you're used to, and that forces you to grow and expand, quickly. You'll do instead of just think, and while you stumble along you'll learn everything you need to know. The knowledge will be alive, tailored to you and your specific needs, as opposed to something you read in a book.

Take the first step. No need to scare yourself stiff; go gently when you need to. But begin.

Make a choice

Maybe you postpone your work because you count on having time later. You will make that dream happen, just not today.

We always have tomorrow, right? Until we don't. Sometimes it takes an encounter with death, a terminal disease or an accident to wake us up from the illusion that there will always be time, later. The truth is, we don't know how much time we have. We can never know for sure that there will be a later. We have this one, precious life, and it is limited both in terms of time and energy. If we want it to be about what matters the most to us, we have to make a conscious effort. We have to make choices, now, in the midst of the mess and too-muchness of it all, because now is all we can ever be sure of.

> "These are the last moments of your life. I can't tell you how long the moments are, but this is it."
>
> GANGAJI

And maybe you're starting to feel frustrated now, because your problem is not that you don't know what you want, but that you want too much! Too many dreams, too little time. You want it all, and you want it right now.

Consider this unwillingness to choose for what it is – resistance. Not the fact that you have many passions, but the unwillingness to choose a place to start. Not choosing is also a choice, one that will either keep you stuck in indecision or lead you to start a million things at once and then fail, inevitably, since no one can do everything at once. Either way, it's a very effective way of keeping yourself from moving forward.

If you had to choose, which of all those dreams would come first?

You don't have to abandon the other dreams; you just need to ask them to form a queue and await their turn, because there's no way you can serve them all at once. There's nothing wrong with being multi-passionate and wanting to create a life or even a business that holds all your loves, but there's no way around the fact that you need to start somewhere. You always need to start with one thing first.

Get specific. And getting specific inevitably means closing

a lot of doors. This can be challenging, especially if you're the type who wants to do everything at once or who likes to keep a foot out the door in case you change your mind. I'm asking you to choose anyway. It will not be a choice for life; your work will grow and take new turns over time, and your focus will shift. But in order to get started, you need to choose. And then go all in with what you've chosen.

Q & A

THESE QUESTIONS about finding clarity and zooming in on your dream come from women who have participated in my courses and workshops over the years. They bring to light the friction and real-life challenges we face as we begin to do this work. Hopefully, reading about their stumblings will help light the way for you.

I feel panic about all the things I want to do before I die

QUESTION: You talk about a sense of urgency and time, how knowing we don't have unlimited time on earth can motivate us to pursue our dreams. That many reach their deathbeds only to regret what they didn't do because they thought they had time and let other things take priority. Interestingly, this is one of the exact reasons I have reached some kind of panic. Earlier this year I felt like I was having an existential crisis—I am keenly aware of my own mortality and that there is so much I want to do with my life, so many things I want to experience, so many ways I want to be of service & inspiration, so many words to write, people to connect with, so much beauty to make. It's spun me into a whirling panic of how to do everything in such a short amount of time, my lifetime.

In order to function and not have a mental breakdown I've had to actually slow down and tell myself that there IS enough time. To trust that there is time. If I didn't believe that I have enough time to do everything that I need to do then I think I would go into a tailspin. I'd love your thoughts on this, Anna.

ANSWER: Good point. I want to clarify a very important distinction: Apply that sense of urgency in order to help you commit to your dream and make it a priority in your life right now. Apply it when it comes to getting clear on what matters most and letting go of the less important. But NOT when it comes to the doing, the actual process of moving your dream from vision to form. Because that process has its own timing. Anything you do to try to rush it will only hurt you and thwart your work.

Whether we have ten books to write in this lifetime or only one is not really in our hands, so we needn't bother about it or feel rushed because we have so much work to do before we die. That's not for us to decide. *We just do the work at hand, one step at a time.*

There's a peace of mind that comes with that. Maybe even some lightness. That's a good thing. Loosening the grip a little will make things so much easier. Makes me think of something actor Paul Newman said. "Always take your work seriously; never take yourself seriously."

It's a paradox. Commit to the work like there's no tomorrow, and then relax into knowing that you have all the time you need.

Love,
Anna

I need recognition!

QUESTION: My creative dream is to be a recognised writer. I've had like a hundred jobs and none of them made any sense to me. The only time I feel free and brave is when I'm writing. I feel like a better person, even. When I'm writing I tend to focus on things outside myself, which is a relief! If I had to save the world, I'd be doing it through writing. But writing is not really DOING, is it? This makes me confused... Is my dream to write a dream of not being in the world? That's a depressing thought.

ANSWER: I hear you say that you are free and brave when you write. You forget about yourself for a bit and turn towards the world around you. You see it in a new light and you write what you see. To me, this doesn't sound like escaping at all, it sounds like participating fully, as who you truly are (a writer). If you ask me, writing is most definitely doing.

I'd like to dig a little deeper into the dream of becoming a recognised writer. There's nothing wrong with wanting to be recognised. But it's important to remember that whether or not you get recognised, by whom, and when, is for the most part out of your control.

Only your writing is fully in your hands. Your actual writing practice. And one part of committing to your writing practice is to recognise yourself as a writer, whether or not anyone else does. Are you with me on this?

What would your dream be if you, for a while, excluded the part about being recognised? I'd like to hear more about this.

Love,
Anna

FOLLOW UP QUESTION: I love when you say that writing can be a way to participate in the world, and that recognition is none of my business. I just do the work I love and then I'll see what happens. It makes sense.

My dream is to write. So, either I learn how not to spend my entire daily quota of energy on my day job, or I need to get a less energy-consuming job so that I can keep up my writing practice.

But my fear is that writing might eventually turn out not to be my thing, after all... What a failure that would be! Some recognition would be helpful. Because, you know, I could have been an experienced social worker or journalist by now, and I'm most definitely not – because all I want to do is write, freely. But what do I have to show for it?

ANSWER: If at some point in your life writing is not your thing anymore, you will know then. Right now it is – you're telling me it is! The strong pull to write that you're feeling is all the information you have for now.

You want recognition, you say. Whose recognition? And how much of it do you want? At what point will you feel recognised enough to know you're truly a writer? When a friend likes your writing? When a teacher approves? When a publisher says yes? When it's a bestseller? When you're writing for a living? What exactly is it that you want?

If you're not absolutely clear on what drives this longing and how to satisfy it, it can very easily turn into a never-ending hunt for more. This is one reason why so many successful artists move through their seemingly successful careers starved, because as long as they're unable to recognise and validate their own work, they don't believe it when someone else does either. In spite of their success they feel unworthy and inadequate, always trying to reach the next level of success and recognition in the hope that it will be enough, that they will finally cross the goal line and feel at ease and at home.

Turn it around instead. Allow yourself to feel at ease and at home in your work first, before anyone else has recognised you. If you can do that the external recognition will, paradoxically, both come easier and matter less.

Courage, dear heart

FOLLOW UP QUESTION 2: I know you're right about the recognition part. I do have problems letting it go. I feel stuck, circumstance wise, and so I dream big without doing much. But circumstances will never be perfect, I know that. Even my kids keep telling me I need to focus. I guess I dream about being a published author because it would mean making money from my books. Then I wouldn't have to spend so much energy on my day job. I could spend my time writing instead.

ANSWER: Wanting to make a living from your craft, instead of juggling a day job as well, is a perfectly valid part of anyone's goal. However, what I point to over and over again is that in order to get there, you still have to focus on getting started in the here and now. Especially in the beginning, your focus must remain with the step-by-step creation of your work, or you will have nothing to make money from in the first place. You see, whichever way we turn, everything keeps pointing us back to doing the work we have before us, right now. Annoying, right? First, become the artist. The person who's doing the work. Then consider money.

Good luck!

I'm unable to choose!

QUESTION: What you said about unwillingness to choose really hit home with me! That it is a form of resistance – not being able to choose, starting too many things, doing too many things at once.

I have dozens of books on craft – how to work subtext, how to write an ending, The Art of Fiction, Writer's Gym, Creating Unforgettable Characters, etc., etc. And stacks of collections of short stories – to learn how others do what I want to do. Have I read them all? No. Do I feel guilty about it? Yes. Do I try to get through them? Yes, but not success-fully. And in the meantime I am not writing my own stories and feeling even worse about that.

My big dream is to have a collection of short stories. My

little dream is to write one every couple of months. But all those books beckon, tempting me with their siren voices, "if only you read us you'll be so much better!!!" And I don't write. What do I do about it?

ANSWER: I think you're absolutely right about this being resistance. In order to be a writer, you need to be a reader. And in order to evolve as a writer, it's helpful to think of yourself as a student. But you already do, don't you? You've devoted yourself to learning your craft in so many ways, and you have been doing so for a very long time.

In order to evolve as a writer, you also need, when the time comes, to let go of the student role and step into your own authority. Your own voice can't be found and expressed while keeping an eye on what you could, should and should not do. You write your way to your voice, trusting nothing but your own guidance in the process.

Maybe being the student is your safe place. If we find safety in learning, we often feel the need to acquire a little more knowledge before spreading our wings. (Just one more degree! One more course!) I think this is the season for you to leave the student aside for a bit, and own who you are. Move those books out of your sight. Move them out of your writing space. I'm serious.

You're a writer. And you tell me know exactly what you want to do. So go ahead and write.

Love,

Anna

CHAPTER 2

Get your priorities straight

"I've seen women insist on cleaning everything in the house before they could sit down to write... and you know it's a funny thing about housecleaning... it never comes to an end. Perfect way to stop a woman. A woman must be careful to not allow over-responsibility (or over-respectabilty) to steal her necessary creative rests, riffs, and raptures. She simply must put her foot down and say no to half of what she believes she 'should' be doing. Art is not meant to be created in stolen moments only."

CLARISSA PINKOLA ESTÉS

WHAT WOULD HAPPEN if you decided to no longer be satisfied with creating in stolen moments only? If you straightened your back and did it publicly from here on. No more hiding. This is your heart's work, whether or not you're currently paid for it. And whatever you dream of calling yourself once you've made it – an artist, a writer, a photographer, a dancer – you can claim it now.

Making such a commitment will bring up all kinds of fears, not to mention shame. Who are you to call yourself an artist? Dear little woman, this is embarrassing, get back in line please!

Bringing this shame to the surface is very useful. We need to know what we're up against. We need to be able to recognise these voices as something we've been taught. We've internalised them, but they're not originally ours. Whose are they? What are they telling you? That you'll make a fool of yourself? That you don't have what it takes? That your family won't approve? That the kids will pay for it? That there's no point? That you'll waste time and money?

For now, just notice what comes up. Simply bringing these

voices into the light will lessen their power. Claiming your identity as an artist – even if it doesn't feel true at first – will create openings for you to move in a new direction.

Where focus goes, energy flows. This is not magic. It simply means that what we devote our attention to regularly will grow to take up more and more space in our lives.

Maybe you can't see yourself as a creative or an artist because your idea of an artist looks so different from what you see when you look at yourself and your life. But if you can't fit into your own idea of an artist, something is wrong with what you've been taught. The idea needs to change. First of all, we need to bring the old stories about The Artist into the light, so that we can see for ourselves all the ways in which they're not true. That's what we're doing here. We question the stories. We claim the right to re-define what a creative person looks like. I know for sure it looks a lot like you.

Actually, there is time

Is your creative work a priority in your life, right now? I don't mean in your thoughts and your dreams, but in your everyday life? Do you give time and energy to it? Does it have a non-negotiable place in your schedule? If not, you'll need to look at your priorities.

Let's start with the most common reason people give for not making their creative work a priority – that we don't have time. Say it enough times and it will become a truth. That certainty makes it very difficult to change. If you're busy defending and justifying your belief that you actually don't have enough time, you can't change. You're too busy being right. That's how you get in your own way.

Yes, it feels like you don't have time. I know. And you probably have less time than a lot of other people. We don't have the same twenty-four hours. A single mother working full time has a much more challenging starting point than a 20-year old with no one to support but herself. The person who carries the heavier burden at home will have less time and definitely less energy than the one who comes home to a set table, and equally, the person with a chronic illness that requires frequent hospital visits and claims a big portion of her daily energy quota will have less time to spend on work than someone who has no health issues. It's silly and offensive to suggest otherwise. "I don't have time" will ring truer for some than for others. But what if it's not the whole truth? Let's just consider the possibility.

Let me borrow an example from the book *The Big Leap* to explain what I mean. We don't refuse to help our kid who just cut her hand and is bleeding on account of us not having time, even though we did decline her invitation to play just a moment ago, with those exact words. Obviously, there was time to be had. It's just that we didn't prioritise play over whatever we were doing, but we did prioritise stopping the bleeding.

If the need is pressing enough, there is time. It's a matter of priorities. And I'm not saying you should ignore your other responsibilities. I'm not saying you should always give your creative work the same priority as a pressing medical emergency (although sometimes, that's what it takes). I'm just asking you to look at how you don't speak the whole truth.

Time thieves

Let's take a look at what we do spend time on, even though we say we have none. Like technology. A recent study shows that Americans now check their smartphones on average fifty two times each day. For those between the ages of eigtheen and twenty four the number rise to eighty six times a day.[7] We have barely begun to understand the ramifications of these new behavioural patterns, but we do know that the effects on human creativity are massive. Research from Florida State University shows that just hearing for instance a social media notification or a text message on your phone will notably affect your mind's ability to concentrate on your work for a long time afterward.[8] And that's from just hearing the notification – not even interrupting your work to respond.

Another study from University of Texas[9] concludes that even having a smartphone nearby reduces available cognitive capacity, because you need to make a conscious and continuous effort not to give in to the temptation of picking it up. Participants in the study who put the phone in a separate room were more effective at completing cognitive tasks.

In our creative work, we need to get below the surface. We need to sink below and beyond our everyday minds to hear the muse as well as our intuition speak. Our devices, it seems, effectively keep us at the surface. They mess with our ability to concentrate and also seem to consume our time to such an extent that we have a hard time making it to our work in the first place.

Also consuming our time are the demands of the beauty industry. Most women spend considerable amounts of time and money on living up to and perpetuating its impossible ideals. Just think of all the work that goes into it – the make-up, the work out, the waxing and shaving, the colouring, blow-drying, styling, the eyebrows, the nails, the toning and trimming of the body, the holding in and filling out, the erasing and enhancing, the moisturising and revitalising, the nip and tuck.

As humans we have been adorning ourselves since the dawn of time; that's not what I'm talking about here. I'm talking about the making of a Woman, the costly, time-consuming and sometimes painful process by which we try to live up to unrealistic and always shifting beauty standards.

Some of the things I mentioned above can be done as part of a healthy and life-affirming self-care routine. They can be everyday rituals that keep you grounded. Working out might make you feel alive and strong. Luxurious crèmes and scented oils might make you feel cared for and nourished. Adorning yourself with make-up or jewellery might please your aesthetic sensibilities, and playing with clothing might make your inner artist happy.

Yes, all that. And we also know that's not the whole truth. This is not a call to stop paying attention to our physical appearances. It's simply an invitation to investigate what we consider mandatory and why. How much time do we spend on playing this game and what are the true rewards and costs? Actually, let me tell you how much time we spend on it. If a woman spends thirty minutes a day on beauty care, she will have spent the equivalent of six years of full time work during her lifespan[10].

I'm looking at these numbers without judgement, because this is not a game we created ourselves. We're conditioned to play by these rules from an early age and there are consequences if we choose not to.

What I can do is question the rules, and I do so more and more as I grow older. I still care what I look like, but now

I'm curious about what human beauty is beyond the learned ideals. What is beauty in an aging body? What is female beauty beyond patriarchal, racist, capitalistic conditioning? I'm curious about a kind of beauty that doesn't require me to constantly change and improve myself.

And I find it worthwhile to ask myself if I really want to spend so much time, energy and money playing a game I never willingly signed up for. The relentless focus on looking thin, pretty and perfect effectively keeps us from turning our attention to our deep needs, to the things that truly matter to us and our wellbeing. Like doing our art. Like changing a sexist world.

"A culture fixated on female thinness is not an obsession about female beauty, but an obsession about female obedience. Dieting is the most potent political sedative in women's history; a quietly mad population is a tractable one."

NAOMI WOLF

Say no, if you can

Most women I know – including myself – find it hard to maintain strong and healthy boundaries. Saying no to other people goes against our learned desire to please, preferably everyone, always. This may sound trivial enough but is actually a survival strategy in a patriarchal society; and historically, even more so.

At times when a woman had no autonomy and little or no say in her own destiny, being able to please other people may have been her only way to try to stay safe. We still do it.

When someone threatens our physical safety, we often resort to trying to placate our aggressor. We don't assert ourselves, usually wisely so because assertion might trigger further aggression. We play small, we smile, we go along in an attempt to get away from harm.

I've seen it over and over again; once women find themselves in a safe environment – or, in the rare case, once we've grown strong enough to disregard the opinion of others – something shifts and we let go of the pleasing and shrinking and playing along. We recognise our own power, and we stop apologising for it. But it requires a deep sense of safety. Our public spaces are rarely safe enough. Women who don't conform to expectations still face resistance, judgement, discrimination and in some cases violence.

"The woman who does not require validation from anyone is the most feared individual on the planet."
MOHADESA NAJUMI

Read the comments on the postings of any assertive and outspoken woman on social media or a news site, especially if she's expressing feminist opinions, and even more so if she for instance is also black or queer or fat. Notice the lengths to which some people – primarily men, but also women who want to maintain the status quo – are willing to go to silence her.

They attack her because she won't follow the rules, won't centre the white, hetero, male story and worldview, won't say yes, won't please. They fear her because she doesn't care about winning their approval any more, and when she doesn't care about their approval, who knows what she might do?

I wish we could all care less. I wish for us to feel safe enough to care less, even outside of our small, women-only

64

spheres, and I totally respect the fact that we don't know how to. Yet.

But we're learning. Practising saying no to what we don't want in our everyday lives is a good place to start. Starting small, saying no to something that won't cause too much of a backlash, noticing that we can in fact survive a little discomfort, noticing that our trust in ourselves grows stronger every time, and that even a small no creates new space in our lives. Space we can fill with things that matter to us.

Who assigned you that role?

In 1955, Anne Morrow Lindbergh explored what it meant to be a woman and a creative in the classic *Gift from the Sea*. She says: "The bearing, rearing, feeding and educating of children; the running of a house with its thousand details; human relationships with their myriad pulls – woman's normal occupations in general run counter to creative life."

She wrote this sixty years ago, but when I read these lines the first time I knew exactly what she meant. "Woman's normal occupations" may have changed and expanded since the 1950s but it's a fact that women are still responsible for family and home to a larger degree than their male partners. There are exceptions to the rule, but for most women this is still the reality. Like Darcy Lockman says, "the traditional pressure for men to be primary breadwinners have lifted but the traditional pressure for women to be the primary caregivers have not lifted".

Sweden is rated at the very top among nations when it comes to equality between the sexes. And still, Swedish working mothers in heterosexual relationships spend on average a full hour more on housework every day compared to their partners.[11] In a week, that's a work day.

A majority of these women also shoulder the role of project leader in the home. We become the spider in the complex and fragile web of family life. We buy gifts, remember birthdays, pack gym bags, keep stock of winter clothes, organise play dates and birthday parties, bake cakes for bake sales, bring the kids to dentist appointments and so on.

Making space for your creative work will mean reassigning some of these duties. And no, you probably can't just drop the ball from one day to the next unless someone else is willing to pick it up (although some of those balls might be okay to just drop and leave lying there). But you can begin to make all that work you do visible. Get very practical about it; make a list and bring it to the table. Don't allow it to be invisible work anymore. Invite your partner aboard and find new, more equal ways to divide these tasks between you. Bring the whole family aboard. Children also need to learn that houses don't clean themselves and mama is not a selfless service institution.

When you do this you might find that your partner won't come aboard. You might find that he prefers things to stay just the way they are. It's heart-breaking to learn that your partner isn't willing to meet you halfway or support your attempt to free up time for something that's important to you. And it's maddening that the responsibility to educate your partner and re-organise the way works should also fall on you, on top of all the rest. It's not your job. You can choose to do it, and it may or may not lead to change. Only you can make that choice, and only you can know if it's worth it.

If you're a single mother, there's no partner to reassign your duties to. For you, maybe it's about asking friends and extended family for more help; maybe it's about taking on fewer responsibilities outside the home because you pull such a heavy load as a parent; maybe it's about becoming really comfortable with "good enough".

It's also a fact that women do more than their fair share at work, including so-called emotional labour. Economics professor Lise Vesterlund's research shows that women in the workforce are more likely than men to: Volunteer to do non-promotable tasks, be asked to do non-promotable tasks, and agree to do these tasks.[12]

We tend to the relational health of the work place, we take on things outside of our area of responsibility; we feel the need to excel instead of stopping at "good enough" – and sometimes for good reasons. Women still need to do more and better to be considered equal to their male colleagues.

We can't change the dysfunctional structures of our work-places single-handedly, just like we can't force our partners at home to change. But we can begin to name what is going on. We can make it visible. We can start to hand responsibilities back to whomever they belong to. We can make different choices and practise saying no.

> "Women have been encouraged to embrace the all-nurturing (many-breasted) role of womanhood as the jewel in the female crown. And while mothering can be a deeply beautiful role, it can also become distorted by self-negation. The Ma-ny-Breasted Mother ends up caring for an array of children, including projects, needs, groups, and persons, that may not even belong at her breast."
>
> SUE MONK KIDD

We can't change the dysfunctional structures of our workplaces single-handedly, just like we can't force our partners at home to change. But we can begin to name what is going on. We can make it visible.

We fear the clarity of a no. We fear how visible our boundaries become. What happens if we are no longer fluid and flexible, always adjusting to the needs and wishes of others? What happens if we stand our ground? Will we still be loved? Will we be safe? This is unknown territory.

Think about all the ways you've learned to fend people off, escape unwanted work or attention, keep unwanted visitors out of your personal space, away from your body, all of it without ever upsetting anyone. Think about the niceties, the politeness, the white lies and the smiling. All the energy that goes into saying no without actually saying no.

A clear no is an art that takes practice, and it is one that we need to prioritise practising. We are going to have to say no a lot more often than we'd like – and a lot more often than others would like, too. We will have to exclude a lot of things from our lives, in order to include the things that matter the most.

Taking it one step further

One aspect of saying no has to do with what we just discussed. Saying no to other people, refusing to do more than your fair share of the work, getting rid of the chores that bog you down. These are often things you actually *want* to say no to, if you could just get past the fear and discomfort. Getting rid of them is a relief.

But then you might find that in order to create time and space in your busy life, you need to say no to things you really like, too. This is difficult in a whole new way. You want to do your creative work, but you also want to go to that concert or to the gym, make time for your friends, travel, go shopping, learn archery, take pottery classes, have two dogs, a beautiful house and still have time left for some Netflix. No wonder we don't get to our work.

Over the last six years, since we decided to leave the city and have our second baby, I've said no to exciting work opportunities; I've said no to exciting travels, to parties, to weddings, to hanging out; I've said no to buying new clothes, to renovating the kitchen, to shiny magazines, to television, to social media.

Honestly, I've been amazed there's anything left. But there is. There's plenty. The more I let go of, the more clearly I see exactly how little fits into a human life.

That's a sobering thought. But it's also empowering. It goes against everything we learn growing up in this culture; the glowing promise that you can have it all, you can do it all, you deserve it all. If only you learn how to multitask, if you become more stress-resilient, manage your time, make the money, put in the hours, shape up, become leaner, faster – you can have it all.

It's not true.

The more of the noise, the distractions and the man-made obligations I remove from my own life, the clearer it becomes. The things that are truly important to us claim all the time and space we have available. Family, friends, home, work, play and expression. Even that is a full plate. Even from that short list, some things will have to give during certain periods of your life. If you or your kid becomes ill, maybe that's all that fits for a long time. If you're starting your own business from scratch, maybe that's all you'll be doing for the next two years.

When we moved from the city, we bought a magical little cottage on the mountainside where I thought I would have this wonderful creative life and write all the books that want to be written. Turns out the beautiful old house required so much work and money it ended up being what kept me from writing – as well as from playing with the kids, spending time with my love, and resting.

It took some soul-searching; but we got clear on what mattered the most and sold the house. It hurt to prioritise that hard. I wanted to keep the house, the big lush garden, the fireplaces and everything I loved about it, just like I want to travel with my loves, have friends for dinner, buy me some pretty things to wear, have a studio and a study and so much more. I want all of that.

But my deeper self? She desires two things and two things only. To love and to write.

Good to know.

"A thousand half-loves must be forsaken to take one whole heart home."

RUMI

In the end, whether you will have time for your creative work or not is a matter of fierce prioritising. What is most important to you? Get clear on it, and do what it takes to make space for it. It will be uncomfortable, it might feel almost impossible, but still – if this is going to happen, you will have to make space for it to happen. No one else is going to.

All the time you want vs. all the time you need

Another important thing to say about time is that we can have all the time we need for this work. But maybe not all the time we want. This is a crucial difference. I know you crave oceans of time. We dream of having all the time in the world, unlimited resources. Just imagine all the things we'd be able to accomplish if we did. Here we go again with the dream of the artist who escapes to his cabin in the woods for months of solitary writing.

That dream is just one more way we keep ourselves from getting started. We don't need all the time in the world; we need just a little right now, enough to get started. And if you feel that's not enough, it's probably because you haven't zoomed in on your dream properly. Maybe you're still trying to grasp more than you can handle. Maybe you're trying to make things happen faster than is possible for you in your current circumstances.

Get real about what your life is like right now. If you have three little ones at home, or if you're working full time and commuting two hours daily, it will affect the size and scope of the dream you can go for right now. That's not a problem, it's just what this season in your life is like, and it will change.

In the meantime, don't compare yourself to others whose circumstances are completely different from yours. Don't compare yourself to that professional artist who has a team of assistants at her beck and call. Don't compare yourself to the guy whose wife takes care of the house and the kids while he goes away to write his novels. Or the single, 21-year-old bohemian with three pieces in her life-puzzle who can stay up all night painting because no one is going to wake her up in the morning.

I remember being so impressed with Virginia Woolf's extraordinary level of productivity. Her prolific writing, all the letters, the articles, her amazing novels. Eventually it struck me. She had servants! She never had to cook or clean. And she didn't have children. Of course she had more time!

Sometimes it feels like I'm using up half my life-force just figuring out what to cook for my family seven days a week. Having someone else do that work wouldn't make everything easy – I'd still have to get my butt in the chair and write – but there is no doubt it would buy me both time and headspace.

If you're a mother, recognise the immensity of that work. Don't pretend you can just squeeze in your creative work next to everything else you manage. This is what society teaches us – that motherhood, parenthood, is not actual work; it's just something we do as we go about life, and something women automatically know how to do. The work of motherhood is grossly undervalued. Don't buy into that.

Get clear and honest about your situation. Change what you can change and zoom in on your dream until it's a size you can get started on; kids, demanding job and all. Creativity thrives in limited spaces and once you get going, you'll be amazed at how much you can create with what little you've got. Having kids taught me a lot about this, and having chronic pain taught me some more. We create in the midst of life, in the midst of the mess, or we don't create at all.

Keep it real

I still feel that my kids get in the way of my work sometimes. When they get yet another cold and my plans are out the window. When I never seem to get enough sleep. Or when I get that phone call in the midst of my writing time, about when I'll come home or where the yellow boots are. It's exasperating to be constantly interrupted and pulled out of my creative bubble. I've dreamt more than once of running away.

But then I heard something that helped shift my perspective. A woman I admire, writer and comedian Mia Skäringer,

Creativity thrives in limited spaces and once you get going, you'll be amazed at how much you can create with what little you've got.

talked about the myth of the Genius and how self-absorbed the male artist is allowed to be. How everyone tiptoes around him, because he can't be disturbed and everything has to be just so, or he can't (won't) work.

She said that bringing her five-year-old to rehearsal actually helped keep her grounded in reality. Sure it would get messy, with lots of interruptions, but the upside was she couldn't get lost in her nervousness or get too precious about details. "No time to stick my head too far up my own ass", in her own words. Instead of ruining her preparations, his presence helped her keep things real.

I thought about the words of Anne Morrow Lindbergh again, the ones I had related to so strongly.

"The bearing, rearing, feeding and educating of children; the running of a house with its thousand details; human relationships with their myriad pulls – woman's normal occupations in general run counter to creative life..."

There's no denying that the unjust division of labour hinders women's creative work, and yes, the distractions of a woman's "normal occupations" do run counter to the creative life as we've been taught to see it. But maybe there are other ways to see it, and other ways to do it.

I am now certain that creativity must not be compartmentalised. We don't step out of the stream of life to do our work; we do it in the midst of life. Yes, distractions are a challenge. As those studies showed, repeated interruptions from our digital devices shift our brains out of creative mode. But we're talking about our lives here, our kids. That's something else entirely.

"There were times when it felt as though my children were annihilating me ... Finally I came to the thought, All right, then, annihilate me; that other self was a fiction anyhow. And then I could breathe. I could investigate the pauses. I found that life intruding on writing was, in fact, life. And that, tempting as it may be for a writer who is also a parent, one must not think of life as an intrusion. At the end of the day, writing has very little to do with writing, and much to do with life. And life, by definition, is not an intrusion."

SARAH RUHL

You may have just a few moments here and there to work with. So be it. Devote yourself proudly and openly to your work in those moments, stay long enough to breathe some fire into your creative baby, and commit to coming back before the embers die out.

Q & A

HELPFUL QUESTIONS about making time and space for your work, from women who have participated in my courses and workshops over the years.

What if I *do* have time, I just don't use it

QUESTION: What comes up for me is something that is difficult for me to face: I have the time. I have SO MUCH TIME. Many people would probably envy the time I have available to me. I've created a life that is not always financially abundant, but it is a life of wide-open space. I've worked to create this, as it's a core value to me. There's actually not much I need to do to open up the time for me to get my creative work done. So what am I waiting for?!

Time is an available resource to me, and one that is under-utilised. If I use it fully as a resource, my life will change profoundly, I'm sure of it. Life seeps in at every moment and I allow it to distract me. Errands, cleaning, and so on.

Am I the only one to have the problem of having enough time, but not using it wisely?

ANSWER: "If I use it fully as a resource, my life will change profoundly, I'm sure of it." Could this be the very reason you don't use it? It's not just the risk of failure that scares us, but the possibility of success and everything that comes with it: being seen, being held accountable, losing some of our favourite excuses, loss of privacy, more demands on our time and attention, attracting people's judgements.

It's probably helpful to explore what aspects of success, growth and expansion you're resisting and why. You value the unplanned time and the abundance of space in your life. Would a stronger commitment to your writing take that away from you? Getting clarity on this will allow you to make more conscious choices and invite some change, in a way that you feel ready to handle.

Love,
Anna

How do you stick with a new way of thinking long enough for things to change?

QUESTION: I have been wondering how you learn to live a new way of thinking or insight? For example, I love your idea of being vision-led to your creative goals rather than propelled by fear, but it's so challenging for me. How do you not slip back to old habits of fear and scarcity?

ANSWER: It's very much a process. It has taken me years to break the habit of pushing and I'm still working on it. These four practices have been game changing for me:

1. I pay attention to how I actually feel, while working. Over and over again, I check in and notice what my energy is like. Am I tense? Have I stopped breathing deeply? Am I worried that the result won't be good enough, or that I won't make it on time? If yes, I relax my muscles, take a deep breath, maybe shake it off, stretch a little and then I return my attention to the work at hand.

I remind myself that whether or not the result of my work will be "good enough" is not something I can judge until it actually is done (and maybe not even then). And whether or not I will make it "on time" is a question I can't answer in advance, so I don't want to waste precious energy fretting over it.

I just return to the only thing that is ever in my power to control – the task before me right now. I stubbornly bring my attention back, over and over again.

2. Related to number 1. I don't get involved with my thoughts. The tricky thing about fearful thoughts is that we feel compelled to deal with them, to "work them out", to

solve the problem in order to be rid of it.

The truth is we have very little power when it comes to changing our thoughts (contrary to popular belief). They come and go as they please. Luckily, we don't need to change them. Only leave them be and return our attention where it belongs – to the work at hand. To our breathing. To our bodies. Stop paying attention to your thoughts and you break their power over you. You may have to remember this a thousand times a day in the beginning. That's ok. Awareness is a muscle. Every time you remember, the muscle is strengthened and peace is restored.

3. I commit to a practice that helps strengthen that awareness muscle, like meditation or prayer. This is crucial. It can be five minutes, but I need to show up fully and pay attention during that time. In that attentive space, I will hear my own intuition speak.

And then I need to act on this intuitive information. Every time I do, I learn to trust it more and more. I learn to trust myself and my ability to do what needs to be done, as well as the powers that support me in this work.

4. I make an effort to really get to know the creative project I'm working on. I want to understand how this particular project wants to be expressed (not just how I think it should be expressed), what the perfect timing looks like, etc. I want to know the soul of it.

Doing a collage helps me see it from a different angle. I meditate and ask for guidance. I do free-writing, paying attention to when something lights up on the page. I use my Tarot decks. Whatever works, really. This way I get really intimate with my work, and I am reminded that it has a soul and a will of its own.

Over the years, I've noticed what happens when I trust only my own powers vs. when I recognise my place as a co-creator, and there's a vast difference. Both regarding result and process. I am not alone in this, and that is the best discovery I've ever made.

Hope this helps,

Anna

Social media is consuming my time

QUESTION: With so many different platforms and channels available where I could potentially share my work, how do I know where to focus my efforts? I can't be everywhere all the time and I feel like I'm spreading myself thin trying. I notice that I'm afraid I'll miss out on something that could be good if I don't give new things a try. But trying to be everywhere is literally consuming all the time I have available for my work. It's absurd, really. I feel scattered and I'm at a point right now where I feel like this is stealing the joy of my creative project. And at the same time, I feel like I can't just turn my back on social media.

ANSWER: A few questions to consider. How do you like to communicate with people? What comes naturally to you? Does social media light you up or leave you scattered? Are you a writer, a thinker, a talker? An extrovert or introvert? Do you prefer daily interaction with others or long stretches of uninterrupted time and space to yourself? Do you even like the online world? Or would you rather get your hands dirty in your garden or kitchen or studio, and use your phone to make calls and nothing else?

These questions will help you figure out what kind of platform for your work that you actually enjoy tending to and playing with.

And when you know the answer – make a choice. Trying to be everywhere and do everything only drains us, plus we end up doing half-assed work. No wonder at all you feel like you're losing the joy! Commit to one thing – one channel, and get real about how much time you have available to spend on it. Bring your focus back to what's truly important here: doing your actual creative work. Your time is a non-renewable resource. So use it well.

Good luck!

Anna

CHAPTER 3

Plan your work

"For the perfect accomplishment of any art, you must get this feeling of the eternal present into your bones — for it is the secret of proper 'timing'. No rush. No dawdle. Just the sense of flowing with the course of events in the same way that you dance to music, neither trying to outpace it nor lagging behind. Hurrying and delaying are alike ways of trying to resist the present."

ALAN WATTS

IF WE GO straight from idea to doing without laying the necessary groundwork – which is what most people do – we will make it unnecessarily difficult to follow through on our plans.

The first step of a sustainable, successful creative process is to zoom in on our dream until it's clear and concrete enough to start working on. The second step is to simplify our lives until there's room enough to work on it. The third step is to break the dream down into doable steps. If you're the impatient kind, this preparatory work might feel like holding yourself back; like chopping up your beautiful dream until there's nothing left of it. And you might struggle to stay motivated and inspired at this point.

This is to be expected. Just as fear is an inevitable part of the creative process, so is this slightly disappointed feeling once you start getting closer to your dream. All of a sudden it's not shiny any more. It's scary – or just plain boring. This is where a lot of us get stuck; thinking maybe we were wrong, maybe this is not what we really wanted after all. And off we go, chasing another rainbow.

This will have us jump from one project to the next, from one dream to the next, like a serial monogamist. Often we tell ourselves that this is what courage looks like. We tell ourselves that we let that dream go because it wasn't really right; we need to get on this new exciting train that just pulled into the station. And we're not going to let fear keep us from making the leap, right?

But more often than not, it's fear that makes us leap. Fear of commitment. At its worst this behaviour becomes a kind of self-sabotage. When we keep abandoning our dreams midway, we throw all our work away, all the time, energy and money we invested in it. We never stick around long enough for it to begin to pay off. This can be a very costly way of living, emotionally, creatively and sometimes financially too. Go through this cycle a few times and you'll find yourself drained of both resources and self-confidence.

Commit to the reality of your dream

Dreams are only shiny from a distance. When we get close, we see things for what they are – multi-dimensional, complex, messy, challenging and gloriously real. I'm not saying that you should never change your mind or that you can't tweak and adjust as you go. You will and you should. I'm just asking you to listen closely to what you're telling yourself at this point in the process. If your interest is waning, if you feel the urge to quit and hop on a new project instead – inquire into that urge. Is it a true call to change direction, or are you just unwilling to do the actual work?

Remember why you started this. Remember when you fell in love with this dream. Can you trust what led you here and hang in a bit longer before you quit? The thing is, when you really commit to your work it will take you where you need to go. The end destination might be some place you can't even see from where you stand now, but you need to follow along to find out. Don't worry about making the right choice. Don't worry about getting it right from the start. Your work will lead the way, if you only get started.

Make it doable

The reason for planning our work properly is to get out of overwhelm and make the dream doable. I'm a lover of the big beautiful vision but I also know that if you want to make it real, you need to break it down into little chunks and make it a matter of one step after another. "Small and humble enough for you to be willing to act on them", in the words of Julia Cameron.

My daughter recently reminded me of this. The process of getting her to clean her room used to follow a very consistent pattern. I would ask her to do it and without too much fuss she headed up the stairs to her room. Then, half an hour later when I went to check on how she was doing, I would find her slumped on the floor, surrounded by piles of clothes and comic books and teddy bears, completely overwhelmed. "I just don't know where to start," she would say, looking forlorn, and I would end up helping her get it done.

Eventually, she came up with the solution herself. When it was time to clean she asked me to make a list for her, writing down everything that needed to be done, one thing at a time. Pick up the comic books, gather the dirty laundry, make the bed, put all the pens and papers back on the desk, and so on. This time, she got it done in fifteen minutes; no overwhelm. It was so simple; I couldn't believe I hadn't thought of it my-

If the size of your dream overwhelms you, break it down into small, manageable steps, and then focus on one step at a time. Almost anything is doable that way.

self. This is exactly what I've been preaching for years. If the size of your dream overwhelms you, break it down into small, manageable steps, and then focus on one step at a time. Almost anything is doable that way.

Plan for the unexpected

When you plan your dream, focus on what you want the process to feel like. Don't get lost staring at the end goal, postponing health, rest and play until you reach it. It has to be sustainable all the way; your planning needs to accommodate all of you and your life, or it will either fail or hurt you.
What do you need for your everyday life to be sustainable? What are the non-negotiables? What keeps you fuelled up and energised? Take this into account when planning your project.

Never make your plans with your strongest self in mind. It's easy to get ambitious and optimistic and squeeze things in where there really isn't room, and then keep your fingers crossed. This approach rarely gets you beyond the first two weeks.

Don't assume that you'll be in perfect health, that you'll get good sleep, that the kids won't catch a cold (or five) or that everything will run smoothly at work. Don't assume there won't be surprises and disruptions along the way. There will be. Life is never as neat as our planning sheets, so make sure you schedule space for changes, delays and adjustments. Make a plan you can stick with even if a few things go wrong.

The more honest and realistic you can be about your planning, the more likely you are to follow through with it. Keep in mind that everything we do come with trails of minor tasks attached. For example, when you make a plan to start going to the gym, you schedule three forty-five-minute classes a week in your planner. But maybe you don't plan for the time it takes to go back and forth to the gym, you don't take into account that you need to make sure the clothes are cleaned and dried in between classes, or that you need to pack your bag, find the water bottle and the shampoo, or that you need to go online and book the class every time.

We tend to ignore these things, because each of the tasks seem so small and insignificant. But things add up. These trails of unacknowledged work are one of the reasons our days seem to be constantly bursting at the seams.

When you plan your creative project, take into account getting your workspace ready. Take into account the time it takes to get back into concentration if you happen to be interrupted (again, keep the smartphone out of your workspace). Take into account the time it takes to buy the art supplies you need, as well as the time it takes to actually plan the work and follow up on your planning. Plan for getting to and fro, plan for the preparations, and always plan for the unexpected.

Perfect timing

We get optimistic about our planning because we want it all done soon. But sooner is not better when it comes to making dreams real. What matters is that we do the work in such a way that we can keep doing it. It needs to be sustainable, or it won't get done. Don't automatically go into deadline mindset. We're not going for as soon as possible here, we're going for perfect timing.

What is doable for you? A one-year plan to write the book

or a five-year plan? Pay attention to your body in this process. Do you feel stress and tension when you look at your planning? Do you feel a sense of spaciousness? These physical responses are usually a lot more reliable than the suggestions of your ambitious mind.

I know, five years is a long time. But does it matter if that's what it takes to get the job done and stay sane in the process? Your mind says it's not worth doing if it's going to take that long. No point in even getting started; you'll be fifty by the time that book is written. True, but you'll be fifty anyway, whether you write the book or not. And I'd rather toast my fiftieth birthday along with my book release than look back five years from now regretting that I never started.

The power of creative habits

The habits you begin to form now will be the container of all your future creative projects. If you have issues with creating structure because you feel it restricts you or because it seems boring and un-creative, I want you to look a little deeper into that resistance. Because it is resistance.

> "Consciously cultivated, habits can be the protective riverbanks that guide the effortless flow of your creative energy."
>
> HIRO BOGA

Structure won't hold you back; habits don't need to be rigid. As long as you cultivate habits that suit you and your life they will help your work to gather and flow, rapidly, in the right direction. They will save you the need to start from scratch every day. You have your plan, you know what to do. The structure is already there and it leaves you free to dive straight into the river of your work. And within that structure, your creative energy will build powerful momentum.

When you find yourself stuck, creating a clear container for your work can help you get out of our own way. One great example of this is when poet Mary Oliver wrote one of her most famous poems, Wild Geese. This poem has been loved by millions, but was actually written as an exercise in rhythm. Oliver gave herself the task of adhering to a certain set of rules regarding verse and rhythm, and while she was busy paying attention to that structure, something else, something brilliant, slipped through.

Scheduling

When do you work? How often? How long? Your answers to these questions will change over time, as your life circumstances change.

I'm a morning person, so I've always liked to make use of mornings for creative work. My mind is lucid, my body fairly rested, my imagination alive from stepping right out of dreamtime. I love to get up and get an hour of undisturbed writing before anyone else is awake.

But since I'm a mother of small children right now, it doesn't always work out. To be honest, most mornings it doesn't. I'm too tired. Or one of the kids wakes up when I try to sneak out of bed. That's ok. It will change. In a few years' time, the kids will be older and I'll be free to use my mornings as I please again.

This kind of long-term perspective is incredibly helpful,

rather than fighting to make it work when it doesn't. As a mother, my priorities are different from my priorities as a creative. I need to find a way to work with both sides.

I never used to be a procrastinator. I could always trust myself to make good use of my time and I didn't need much in terms of structure to get things done. This has changed over the years, much to my dismay, and I find myself needing more structure, more support, more accountability to get my work done. Maybe it's simply due to my life becoming more complex as my family has grown. Maybe it has to do with the effects on my brain of rounds of exhaustion and burnout. Whatever the reason, it has taken a lot of getting used to.

When I dive into a longer writing project now, I need a long-term plan as well as a daily plan. Ideally I also find a friend working on a creative project and we do weekly check-ins for accountability. I don't always deliver but just keeping the conversation about my work alive helps me take it more seriously.

Writing at the same time every day also helps. If I were to decide on a day-to-day basis if and when I feel like writing, I wouldn't write. I know this because I tried it. Resistance sets in and other things turn into priorities. When there's a certain time scheduled every day, I don't have to think about it – I just get myself to the desk and sit down.

It's not a question of whether I feel like writing or not; it's simply about getting to an appointment on time. And once I get myself to the desk, the rest will work itself out.

If possible, find a special place where you do your work. It doesn't have to be a studio or an office; it could be a table in your favourite café or at the public library. For many of us it's the kitchen table when the kids are asleep. But if you can find a corner of your home that you can devote properly to your creative work, this will be helpful.

Anything and everything we can do to make our work easily available to us is a good idea.

Help yourself focus

Learn to honour the time you've carved out for this work. Use it for this work only; don't start your precious hour by answering a phone call from a friend about something completely unrelated, or by paying a few bills before getting started. This is so damn important. Respect your own planning.

Much is decided in how we deal with and minimise distractions – those we can minimise. Sit somewhere quiet if you need quiet to focus; remove your smartphone from your workspace; tell your family that you are not to be disturbed. (Your kids will disturb you anyway, but if you stick with it they'll eventually get the message).

Since I do most of my writing on my computer, there's always the temptation to check email or dive into that bit of research on my to-do list. It's just the click of a button away. But as much as possible, I want to stick with the writing and only the writing for the assigned time. If something comes up along the way I can scribble a note about it on a piece of paper or in a separate document on the computer, just to get it out of my head.

To keep from giving in to these impulses it helps to sit in a place where I don't have access to the internet. But that doesn't happen often these days, and anyway we bring those damn phones everywhere so that's that. Another solution can be to use some of the software available to block certain sites on your computer for a certain time.

Using software to keep you from logging on to Instagram may sound ridiculous. Do we really have to treat ourselves like children and lock away the candy? The answer is often yes. We do. Our creative work is vulnerable, unknown, challenging, sometimes difficult, sometimes tedious and never-ending. It's hard work. Of course we'd rather watch Netflix or scroll through the easy beauty of our Instagram feed instead.

> "I would put chocolate in my studio and say, 'You know, Nat, there's this chocolate you can have if you get over there.' And usually if I got over there, I would start writing. Sometimes I need to get out of the house and go to a café and write. Sometimes I'll write with other friends to get myself going. And sometimes I just say 'Ok, Nat, enough. Go one hour. Keep your hand going.' I'll do whatever it takes."
>
> NATALIE GOLDBERG

Whatever it takes. If you work better when there's a reward waiting for you at the end of your hour, go for it. Chocolate, an episode of your favourite series, whatever works.

Just don't make it too complicated. If you can't work unless the moon is in a certain phase or the whole house is cleaned first, your habits might be hindering rather than supporting you. Keep it simple. Find some small thing to help you get to your work. Chocolate is great. A favourite teacup, that hat you like to wear when you paint, or the incense you burn. Whatever gets you into the right mood quickly. Some creatives steer clear of any such habits, not wanting to be thrown off course if that teacup breaks or they can't find the hat. But I trust you to be able to handle it. The advantages of creating these little fast-lanes into work mode outweigh the rather small risks.

Be prepared to go a few rounds with yourself about your new habits. You will resist them to begin with; it's to be expected and it's ok. Just stick with it; come back if you lose track, and adjust as you go. Habits grow stronger over time.

Q & A

HELPFUL QUESTIONS about planning and structure, from women who have participated in my courses and workshops over the years.

What are your creative habits?

QUESTION: May I ask what your daily creative practice looks like? Do you reserve a time each day to write or create? Do you have an on-going project that you return to, in order to make use of a smaller window of time? Is it visible to your family?

ANSWER: I've shaped a business around my creative work, which means there are a million things to attend to besides the actual creative work. It's easy to get lost in the running of the business, to the point of forgetting why I started it in the first place.

It's an on-going commitment to make time and space for it. I need space for being a visionary, a creative and a writer, not just a business owner. Sometimes this means I have to say no to lucrative projects or to tempting collaborations in order to make time, which is incredibly difficult. But mostly it just means recognising it as necessary work and scheduling accordingly. There's always ten minutes. There's always some time during a week that can be devoted to this. If I don't, both my creative self and my business will suffer.

In order to make space for my creative work, I try to keep my life as simple as possible. I have very few commitments outside of family, health and work. I prioritise these three areas over everything else, with very few exceptions. Using the word "no" frequently and firmly is absolutely necessary.

Yes, I move in and out of projects; some days I have 20 minutes for a writing project and it doesn't sound like much, but if the project is "alive", meaning if I attend to it regularly, it's right there waiting for me and 20 minutes is plenty. (And sometimes I stare at the blank screen for 20 minutes, getting nothing done.)

And yes! My creative work is visible to my family. I talk about my creative projects with my kids and when I take a couple of hours on a Sunday to write, I tell them I'm going to write. This is important. We want to show our daughters that it's possible to be an artist AND a mother. We want to show them what commitment looks like, and that it's ok and allowed to prioritise our dreams in this way, as a woman. It doesn't mean that we're leaving or bailing out of our family life. Just that we can and will do both.

So, basically my creative routine comes out of having my priorities straight and then showing up for my work in a way that works for my family and me. Over time, I tweak and adjust my schedule and habits, until they feel effortless and supportive (or until the kids' routines change and I have to start right over again).

Good luck!

Anna

How do I stop resisting structure?

QUESTION: I feel like a terrible planner! In some ways I've embraced this. For instance, as a mother, I know that I might at any moment simply want to stay home with my child and rest, bake cookies, watch movies, or play cards. So in general, I keep us as commitment-free as possible. Because who knows how we will feel tomorrow, or the next day? I've spent a lot of time getting to this place – a lot of learning to say no and a lot of prioritising rest and down time. It's really paid off and our lives are very spacious and "chill", for lack of a better term.

However, this "chill" quality seems to be getting in my way when I'm trying to create new creative habits. I struggle creating structure for myself. When someone else gives me a project with a deadline, I wrestle a little bit with getting started, but once I do, I'm extremely efficient and motivated. I am really, really good at getting things done once it's in a clear container and timeline.

I feel like I am under-utilising myself. My goal right now is to write (anything) for 1-2 hours a day. I have other dreams, of course – books to be written, e-courses and so on – but for now, I want to focus on just creating my craft. And I'm resisting the scheduling. I think it may help me to buy a nice planner and also to create specific places for my writing – a new notebook that I love, and also a specific and new place on my computer for any digital writing that I do.

I've also just gotten a part-time office job. There are a few reasons for this, but the primary one is that truly I've been dying for structure and I'm struggling creating it for myself. Some of my most creative and productive times have actually been when I've had a job working for someone else. I think having this job and this commitment will help me. We will see. But I definitely need to work on my scheduling avoidance and on being more creative with how I approach this. Any advice is welcome.

ANSWER: This spacious quality that you have cultivated in your life allows you to go with the flow and be spontaneous, and it's so valuable. It seems to be something very central to your wellbeing. But the way I see it is that it needs to be balanced with periods of focused and structured work, or it will eventually lose that relaxed quality and become some-thing else (avoidance, stagnation). Flow needs to be directed or it will lose speed and power quickly. I think that's why you feel under-utilised.

About your resistance to structure. Maybe you prefer the

dreamy, open spaces of the big abstract vision. You know, the realms of potential. It's a tempting place to be, very far from the challenges and heartaches of the day-to-day work of making a dream real. If so, what is it you gain by staying there? What is it you avoid?

Another aspect: You say that you have no problem getting things done for others "once it's in a clear container and timeline". And this makes me think that your current goal of "writing anything for 1-2 hours a day" is probably not a clear enough container for you.

First of all, writing for two hours is a long time, especially if you don't even know what you're going to write. What if you do half an hour to begin with? This will give your resistance less fuel.

And see if you can decide to focus on some small doable project – either one that you can finish in one sitting, like a poem, or something that you can work on for a few weeks, like an essay or a short story. This could make it easier to get to work. All that open space might simply be too daunting.

Then you decide how long you plan to keep up this writing-half-an-hour-a-day routine. One month? A year? Knowing this will help your mind relax.

And then you decide where you are going to write – where you are going to sit and what notebook you're going to use, or what file if you write on the computer. Holding space for your work like this will make it easier to just show up.

This will create a sturdy container for you. What will you write? For how long will you write? Where will you write? Try it out and see how it goes.

Love,
Anna

What do I do with all the "what ifs"?

QUESTION: I have a really clear goal now and it feels so good to focus on that goal. It has all kinds of sub-goals, and they are easy to split into small steps. I've made a very clear list of what needs to be done and I know I have the time, support and resources to really do it. On the one hand this makes me feel relieved and happy because WOW, I am going to be able to pull this off before the crazy summer seasons starts! On the other hand it overwhelms me because of all kinds of "what ifs".

What if I can't do it? What if inspiration and creativity won't come when I need them? What if I don't make this deadline and this project will fall behind because of the very busy summer season? What if by then I won't have this energy and motivation anymore? What if what if what if. What do I do with all these what ifs?

In order to stay out of overwhelm, I've decided to plan just one thing per day, or, if they are smaller tasks, a maximum of three. That way it all stays manageable. Except for the noise in my head ...

ANSWER: Yes, this sounds totally doable. I love that you have scaled your project down to one or just a few simple steps each day, this will really help you stay out of overwhelm.

And what if things don't go as planned? Yes, what if you drop all of those what ifs and come back to what is, instead? :) Come back to the one small step ahead of you, as that is the only thing you have any control over. You'll need to remind yourself of this a million times a day, probably, as your mind is so used to taking off into the future. Gently bring yourself back, over and over again. Feel your two feet on the floor. Stay in touch with your body, it helps immensely.

Also, see if you can start to cultivate a little trust in the dream itself. You are not required to make all of this happen by your own power only; you join your power with the (massive) power of this dream and together you make it happen. It's a co-creation process.

You don't have to push anything into happening. All you have to do is your part of the work; the tasks you've planned, one after the other. It will get you where you need to go, and all in perfect timing too.

Love,
Anna

CHAPTER 4

Use your fear

"The speaking will get easier and easier. And you will find you have fallen in love with your own vision, which you may never have realised you had. And you will lose some friends and lovers, and realise you don't miss them. And new ones will find you and cherish you. And at last you'll know that only one thing is more frightening than speaking your truth. And that is not speaking."

AUDRE LORDE

ULTIMATELY, WE CAN prepare and plan all we want, but it's in the doing that it's all decided. Because it's in the doing that resistance sets in. Fear takes the stage, and if we don't know how to deal with it, it might scare us right back into hiding, indecision and procrastination.

We may experience resistance as a sense of unworthiness and self-doubt. We may experience it as perfectionism and fierce self-criticism. We may experience it physically, as tension and restlessness. It may show as procrastination, indecision or a sense of vagueness, as if we are not quite sure what we're doing or where we're going. Or it may feel like indifference, seeping into our minds like poison.

Who are you to do this work? a voice in our head asks. What does another story or painting or song matter? It's all been said and done anyway (better than you could ever hope to do). And beneath these voices is profound fear. Of being seen, being judged, being found not good enough or maybe too good, too much, too powerful.

The voice of fear sounds different for everyone, but there are also common themes related to gender, class, race and so on. It's useful to recognise this. In what way is fear culturally shaped? What do female creatives risk that male creatives do not?

Fearlessness is privilege. The archetypal fearless artist is a white male. He disregards safety. If needed, he downs a glass of single malt, headbutts the fear and gets on with it.

He can afford to. He already has space to roam free in this world; he can go to excess and still be safe. He's challenged or threatened by very few situations or people.

This is not the case for women. A woman only needs to walk home alone late at night for it to become clear how far she is from roaming free. We don't own this world. Considering the statistics of how often we are raped, abused and attacked, we don't quite own our bodies either.

In her memoirs *Minor Characters*, beat writer Joyce Johnson describes how one of her Barnard professors told her and her female classmates that if they truly wanted to be writers,

they wouldn't be wasting their time in a classroom, but be off traveling America on a freight train searching for something worth writing about. What he conveniently ignored was the fact that a life "on the road" was infinitely more dangerous for a woman than for a man. He also failed to recognise that for a woman in America in the fifties, attending a university class in pursuit of a writing life, instead of getting married and having children, was as brave a venture into the unknown as any roadtrip across the continent.

Some fears are our minds playing tricks on us. Some fears are real and justified. "Feel the fear and do it anyway" is simply not adequate advice. We need tools, not pep-talks. Tools that actually work.

What is fear?

The physiology of fear gives us the clues we need to develop these tools. To put it very simply, our brains can be divided into three main areas of function: the instinctual brain; the social/emotional brain; and the executive brain.

The instinctual brain is the oldest, most primitive part of our brain. It's located at the base of the skull, and it regulates our basic bodily functions and threat-avoiding impulses. Its primary function is to keep us safe.

The social/emotional brain is a newer structure, overlaid on top of the instinctual brain, and this is where emotional processing, memory and connection to others happen.

The executive brain is the most recently-evolved region of the brain; it is overlaid on top of the emotional brain and it regulates thought and higher function. This is the part of the brain that differentiates us from other species and it grows and develops as we hone particular skill-sets. This is where all our thinking, learning, problem-solving and creating happen.

Each of these systems is integrated into the next one, and what is important for us to know is that the lower structures control access to the upper ones. Each level is a gate to the next.

Once our survival is accomplished or restored, the lower brain opens the gate to the midbrain, and once connection is accomplished or restored, the midbrain opens access to the upper brain, which then makes creativity and learning possible.

But if the lower brain does not perceive our survival as accomplished or restored, it will not open the gates. It means that in order for the brain to access its full creative capacity, we first need to feel safe, secure and emotionally connected.

Thus, we are looking at an incredibly important and overlooked aspect of the creative life – Safety. Which is something quite different from headbutting your fears.

What you need in order to feel safe will depend on your life circumstances, your personality, your life story and so on. If you're a highly sensitive person, as many creative people are, this goes into the equation. If you have a history of trauma, you might need to work even harder to find that solid sense of safety, and this work will often involve getting professional help. But it can be done. I know it can be done.

A losing battle

And it needs to be done, because whatever your starting point, there's no getting around fear in the creative process. When you stretch and grow, fear will come. But feeling afraid doesn't have to be a problem; not if we know how to deal with it. It's when we fight the fear that we end up lost. When we try to numb it or ignore it or change ourselves so that we won't have to feel fear in the first place. Fear is inevitable. It is a signpost, marking the old borders of your comfort zone. It's our companion on this path.

When fear tugs at your sleeve, it's trying to get you to pay attention to what is to come. "If you are going to grow beyond this point," it says, "you will face the unknown. Things will change. Are you sure it's safe to continue?" (Although let's be honest, to the untrained ear it sounds a lot more like "Run!!!")

This is where most of us back off, abandoning our dream because we don't have an answer to that question. We don't know if it's safe and we don't know how to make it safe either. Some of us ignore the fear and push on through, which always requires some level of numbing out. And when we numb out we make bad decisions. When we abandon our sensitivity we also abandon our inner navigation system and we end up lost, one way or the other.

What would happen if we neither backed off nor pushed forward? What if we looked at fear as our signal to pause and tend to our needs?

What is it that you're about to face on the next stage of this journey? Change and growth always involve some level of disruption. Things might get shaken up. Not everyone will approve. What do you need in order to feel safe enough to move forward anyway?

Never mind the tenth step, or the ninetieth. Right now, right here, what do you need? This is one of the most important questions you can ask yourself, ever. In your everyday life as well as in your creative work.

Inhabiting your body

We all have go-to strategies to soothe ourselves; simple things that calm our whole system and bring us back to our senses. Mine always involves kindness and breathing, often moving my body as well.

The tricky thing about our brain is that it reacts to illusory threats just as strongly as to actual threats. That's why the first step is always to connect with the present moment, so that you can find out for yourself if your survival is actually threatened. It usually isn't, even though you just published a vulnerable blog post.

You connect with the present moment through your body. Let's call this grounding. Fear is a hot air balloon; it lifts us

The Power of now

114

out of the present moment, out of our bodies. A grounding practice helps you settle right back, feet on the earth, in touch with your senses and the reality of the moment.

It's not complex. It doesn't require special equipment. You don't need to take a class or find large chunks of time. Just a moment here and there and the discipline to actually do it.

"That's too simple; it won't work," your mind might whisper, urging you to look for some more advanced, time-consuming remedy. Preferably one complicated enough to give you a reason to postpone and procrastinate some more.

Because how can a few deep breaths or a moment of body awareness affect such strong, primal feelings and reactions?

Fear disconnects us from the higher functions of the brain. The antidote is "simply" to re-connect. It doesn't solve the issue – whatever triggered your fear to begin with. But it brings you back to a place where you're capable of solving it, or where you realise there's nothing to solve in the first place.

As a wise woman once said – "Did you know that 10-20 minutes of meditation per day can significantly reduce your risk of giving a shit?"

This is very good news.

One step at a time

You don't need to fix your fear once and for all. In fact, you can't. That's not how humans are wired. You just handle what's in front of you right now and leave the rest for later.

One step at a time; that's all you ever need to master. If you've planned your work properly, one step, one day, one week at a time is all you ever need to worry about.

If the thought of your end goal freaks you out, come back to the present moment. Come back to today's work, to the task at hand. This you can handle. This is all you need to handle.

If the thought of your end goal freaks you out, come back to the present moment. Come back to today's work, to the task at hand. This you can handle. This is all you need to handle.

The truth is, you know very little about the end goal of your journey anyway, or who you will be when you get there. The reality of creative work is that you will often need to act before you're even sure of what you're doing. But your soul knows; your gut feeling tells you you're on the right track. And each step you take grows you into the person who is able to take the next step, and the next.

We make the path by walking it. Information will often be given on a need-to-know basis. Your job is to find ways to stay safe and present and allow your work to take shape, one step at a time.

The shitty first draft

Fear will come at different stages of the creative process for different people. But one stage that trips most of us up is the first draft stage. Whatever your line of work is, there is an equivalent of a shitty first draft. That first rough version, somewhere between blueprint and finished product. It's a skeleton, and it doesn't resemble what you had in mind when you started. At all.

When you're a writer, the first draft is the first finished version of your manuscript. It's complete with a story line, characters, a beginning and an ending. But apart from that, nothing is finished about it. The dialogue is embarrassing, the antagonist is flat and there are large gaping holes in the narrative. This is the stage when my writer clients call me and say, "This is not going to work. I obviously can't write. No one can ever see this."

For most creatives, producing the finished first draft is the most difficult part of the process. Mainly because we don't allow it to be a first draft. We can't stand how shitty it is, so we keep interrupting the process, keep backing up, picking it apart, deleting, editing, instead of moving forward.

It's easy to get stuck there, tweaking and polishing and trying to perfect something that is not meant to be perfect.

It's only meant to be a sketch, a beta version – your warm-up. It's the necessary step between idea and finished result. We cannot go straight from vision to perfect execution. The gap is too wide; we must bridge it somehow, and the first draft is our bridge.

But in order for it to function as a bridge, we must allow it to take shape in the first place, without constant interruption. We must endure its imperfection and watch it unfold with as much curiosity and openness as we can muster, so that we can learn what we need to know to then take it from draft to finished creation.

Needless to say, the inner critic and perfectionist will have a hard time with the first draft stage. They will panic at the sight of this rough creation and they will judge us, shame us and criticise us relentlessly. They will do whatever is in their power to stop us from moving forward, and the best way is to convince us to stop creating and start polishing and fussing with the first draft instead.

Let them steer the ship, and you will not get past this stage. Or you will get past it, but it will be a painful drag every time. Eventually you will start to dread it. Which is sad because this stage is meant to be the true adventure of the creative process.

Get back on the playground

The first draft is your playground. This is where you get to try things out, make wrong turns, try again, re-consider, and create without the pressure of perfection. It is allowed to be crappy.

The trouble is, from early in our lives, women are bombarded with messages about how we need to be perfect in the eyes of others. Always look good, never embarrass ourselves, never make mistakes. This doesn't exactly make for a playful approach to life.

It makes me think of when I was thirteen and my friend and I were hanging out with some guys from school. They were on a trampoline, jumping, making flips and laughing. My friend and I stood next to the trampoline, watching. I remember how I kind of wanted to be up there too, but there was no way I was going to, in front of these slightly older guys, one of whom I had a crush on. No way I was going to jump around and get all sweaty and red-faced, and lose control of my clothing, being looked at by them from every possible angle.

Just the week before, a couple of older guys had jokingly made some really hurtful remarks about what my female classmates and I looked like – or rather, what our asses looked like – standing in the starting blocks in track and field class. That humiliation burned clearly in my memory as I watched them fool around on the trampoline.

One of the boys asked us to come and join them, but we kept declining until he shrugged and went back to jumping, saying to his friend "Girls don't know how to have fun."

I don't remember what I responded, if I responded; but I remember the feeling of unfairness. I was thirteen and I already knew it was really important for me to look good to these guys; to all guys in fact. I knew it was a lot more important than having fun. I was also aware that the rules were different for us than for them, even though I didn't understand why.

I've spent another thirty years unlearning that "truth". I've had to learn to play again, to risk looking foolish (and ugly and unsexy and red in the face and whatever), to allow myself to make mistakes and not take everything so seriously, to just try things out and see how it goes, to do things simply because I feel like it, and – this is a big one – even if people are watching.

The creative process requires all of this and more. We can't make dreams happen if we won't allow ourselves to look foolish and make mistakes. Because we will make mistakes. For sure.

We dream of a formula that will save us the discomfort and humiliation of failure. But what if failing wasn't connected to our self-worth? What if trying and failing and learning and trying again was simply the expected and natural trajectory of a creative life? A discovery process that we could begin to get curious about instead of terrified by.

Since I started this work, I've failed more times than I can count. I've spent money I didn't have, teamed up with the wrong people, I've under-delivered, launched things that tanked, been rejected, messed up professional relationships, tried to be someone I'm not, dropped important balls, sent emails to the wrong person and generally made an ass of myself.

Thanks to all of that, I have some business smarts now. I didn't before. I know the ups and downs of the creative process intimately, so much so that I can teach it. I didn't before. I know a whole lot about self-care and all the craziness that happens if you don't do it. I didn't before.

My point is that failing taught me most of what I know. I

We need to see other
women play and fail and
mess around a lot more
in order to learn that
it's okay and allowed.
We need to see enough
of it for us to begin to
experience it as normal.
The new normal.

still don't like it when it happens but I've come to accept that there's no way around it. This is how to learn and grow; we get in the arena and start practising.

Sometimes this is easier when you are surrounded by women only. I'm always amazed by how daring and playful women can become, how deep their laughter, how irreverent their jokes, when in the company of women they trust. Even the Good Girl might be persuaded to make a little mess if she feels safe enough.

Ask yourself that question again. "What do I need in order to feel safe enough to move forward?" Find spaces and people you trust, and start there. Fail on small projects first. Expand at a pace you can handle.

The fears you face are uniquely yours, and they're also our collective fears. By challenging them, we create more and more space – both for our creative selves and for the young girls following in our footsteps. We need to see other women play and fail and mess around a lot more in order to learn that it's okay and allowed. We need to see enough of it for us to begin to experience it as normal. The new normal.

Who's in charge?

If you want to transform the creative process from battlefield to playground it helps to become aware of the different parts of you that are at work at different stages of the process.

You need to employ different parts of you for different tasks. Your critical and analytical abilities will come in handy when editing a text, for instance, or when planning a marketing cycle. But in the early stages of creating, in the first draft stage, you need intuition, not analysis. You need openness, not certainty. You need to be the beginner all over again, to learn anew, to look at everything with fresh eyes. Here, you're not in control and you don't need to be.

The trouble is, most of us are trained to rely on our factual and analytical minds to such an extent that we have trouble letting it stand back. There's that ol' patriarchy speaking again. Analytical, rational, factual, critical, in control = good. Intuitive, receptive, emotional, open = not so good.

But we can re-learn. We can first of all learn to notice when the analytical, critical mind is trespassing into the territory of the playful, messy creative, or the territory of the receptive intuitive; and when that happens, we can learn how to pause, re-group and start over.

Equally, we can notice when the pendulum swings too far in the other direction and we linger in the emotional, open, intuitive space even when it's time to call in the rational mind and get about our business.

One is not, as we've been taught to believe, better than the other. Both are needed, just for different purposes. We've also been taught to believe that men occupy one end of the spectrum and women the other. The truth is, whatever our starting point, all of us can learn to move along the full spectrum, and I believe we need to in order to do our work justice.

A good grounding practice is useful here. It will bring you back into the body and into the present moment, from where you can make truer, kinder and better choices.

Q & A

HELPFUL QUESTIONS about fear and resistance, from
women who have participated in my courses and workshops
over the years.

What if I follow my creative dream at the expense of someone else?

QUESTION: When I was eigth years old, we moved to a new place and I had to change schools. When I crossed the schoolyard for the first time, I remember someone yelling "You know what? Your grandfather is in our classroom." Above the blackboard in that room were three portraits of famous writers.

For several years, I wrote essays and did dictations under the strict eyes of my grandfather, looking down from a black-and-white photo on the wall. His books were translated into more than 40 languages and sold millions of copies. My late grandmother, his wife, is considered one of the most success-ful poets of her time. Two Bohemians, living a dream life in the countryside, close to nature, with Arab horses under old apple trees and long walks in the woods. They gathered the most inspiring artists, musicians and writers around their kitchen table.

While their style of writing was and is loved by many, while both had a great talent in telling stories and capturing moments, and while their way of living has been a source of inspiration for many, their family paid a high price for their dream. Their children grew up with neglect, and physical and emotional abuse; and they passed it on to the next generation, to me, to my siblings, to my cousins. They also passed on a culture of concealment, because nothing, noth-ing may ever stain a famous name.

So today, when you asked me about what would be the worst-case scenario if I allowed myself to go fully for what I truly want, these thoughts came up. How much is someone else expected to pay if I allow myself to go for my dream? How much space am I entitled to take? What if fulfilling my own dream will make me blind to the dreams and needs of someone else? It is not the lack of money or the thought of being unsuccessful that is my worst-case scenario, it is that blindness, that ruthlessness I am afraid of. I want to trust myself more, to feel more courageous. I want to hear my true voice and learn to distinguish creative need from creative greed, and not let someone else pay for what is important to me.

ANSWER: Thank you for sharing so openly and courageously. You're breaking the legacy of silence and concealment when you do.

"How much space am I entitled to take?", you ask. This question is important, because it speaks to the stories you carry and the rules you've decided to follow. The obvious answer would be "as much as you need". But you're never going to claim as much space as you need if you believe it can only happen at the expense of someone else's space; that you can only make your own voice heard by drowning out someone else's voice. As long as that story feels true for you, you're going to hold yourself back.

This pattern has been passed down through generations in your family. You've taken on the important work of breaking the chain. This is necessary and good but also very difficult, as I know you know. This is multi-generational trauma at play and it could be that you need professional help resolving it.

I'm curious to hear what you find when you explore your creativity as a benevolent force, a life-giving force, contributing to the good of all, through you. Instead of the consuming, destructive, selfish force represented by your grandparents' way of life. Because it is a benevolent force. Whatever went wrong in the way your grandparents chose to live their lives did so because of who they were and the choices they made, not because of their creativity.

If you can begin to break the connection you've made between a creative life and ruthless behaviour, it will free up enormous amounts of energy and space for you, but probably also a whole lot of grief. Let this process take time and make sure you seek support when you need it.

Love,

Anna

What is this fuss about safety?

QUESTION: I've been thinking – is safety really something to strive for as a writer? I have read so many books exhorting me to push boundaries, to be fearless in my writing. Anne Lamott, Annie Dillard, Natalie Goldberg, even that old coot Hemingway all say the same thing – be bold, don't be afraid, go for broke and don't look for safety nets. That only by becoming fearless will I be true to my own self and my creativity. That only that way will I be able to write good, new, exciting and innovative work.

This focus on safety seems to go against all the writerly wisdom I have come across till now.

ANSWER: I love this question. I think the writers you mention are right. We do need to risk it all to express ourselves fully. We do need to give it our all and not hold back.

But that's not the same as being fearless. Fear comes when we step into unknown territory. It's a given. It's how humans function. And it's not a problem as long as we learn how to keep moving forward, alongside the fear.

When we do, when we learn how to stay present and

connected in the face of what's scaring us, we are sometimes graced with moments of true fearlessness. It's a blessing when it happens. Fearlessness is the result of knowing, for a moment, that we are absolutely safe, *even as we risk falling*. We realise that what others think of our work truly doesn't matter, that whether or not we are successful is not in our hands, and that no matter what will come of it, doing the work is worth it.

This willingness to face whatever may come depends a lot on your ability to take care of yourself. You need to have your own back first. You need to listen to your needs and meet them, to stretch and grow at a pace you can handle. The moment you push yourself too far, your fears will snap back and hit you over the face like a rubber band.

What do you need in order to feel safe? What do you need to feel safe enough – as a human, as a woman and as a creative being – to go for it? To dive in, to go for broke? What does safety look like to you, in your process and in your life? Get interested in these questions, because the answers will help you become the free and courageous writer you yearn to be.

Without rooting into our own being like this, few of us ever make it to fearlessness. We can claim to. We can do the "fearless artist" pose (and then turn to our drug of choice to keep the fear in check). But that's something entirely different.

Go gently,
Anna

What if I'm kicked out the pack?

QUESTION: I'm working on my fears right now and this is what's coming up. If I go fully for my creative dream, I fear losing connection to the world, to people I love; I fear being labelled as an outcast of sorts. This is a huge fear.

Are there female lone-wolves? See, I was always such a pack-person. I'm still terrified of losing connection. I've worked so much and so hard on being more myself, trusting my own strength – which I also fear, because I know it can destroy. I can destroy. I have so much power, I often both under- and over-estimate it.

Anyway, I don't think I do well as a lone-wolf. Not for long, anyway. I've learned to enjoy solitude and time alone, but, again, I need the balance. My deepest fear is just being chucked out of the pack.

So, this is where I am. If anything comes to your mind when reading this, I'd appreciate your comments.

ANSWER: Are there female lone-wolves? For sure. Here's one writing to you. But a wolf is also a pack animal, just like a human, and each of us needs our own particular balance between solitude and connection. No one is fully either one or the other.

What I know is that if you stick with the pack for fear of being alone, you will not find true connection or safety there, because the connection will be conditional; always tainted by your fear of being ostracised. If you behave like this, will it be acceptable to the pack? If you move like this, work like this, speak like this, will you still be allowed to stay? This is not belonging; this is fitting in, and fitting in always requires us to change and adjust ourselves to something other than what we are.

Not until you're willing to risk your place in the pack for the sake of being loyal to your own heart will you find a sense of true home, both in yourself and in the pack. *You cannot claim your space in the pack until you claim your right to be who you truly are in that space.* And this is a life's work.

That said, the fear is real. I don't want to belittle what you're up against. You mention both fearing and craving your own power and this is a big one. Female power is still controversial and most of us have been taught to make ourselves smaller in order to fit in and be accepted.

It's probably helpful to take a look at what messages you've received about this, growing up – both implicit and explicit. In what way is female power allowed to be expressed in your family? Among your friends? In the society you live in? In what way is it criticised or even forbidden? And if you zoom in a little more, what is it about your creative dreams that you fear might get you kicked out of the pack?

Courage,
Anna

What if I give it my all and it's still not enough?

QUESTION: I have totally embraced the idea that fear is a reminder that my boundaries are shifting. And for me, fear manifests itself in control. I know I am fearful of the next creative step when I need to pull everything out from the pantry and clean it properly. Or when the kids' bedrooms seem so overwhelmingly messy that I ignore everything else to sort their clothes into neat, colour-coded piles. Clearly, the uncertain path ahead sends me into a spin, and to my fearful self, the only way through it is order.

Where I am stuck is with my first book. I wrote it four

years ago. On and off, I have been polishing it ever since then, and I'm working with a writing mentor now. I agree with all her suggestions, and I know I need to go deep to solve some structural problems. Some of the storyline seems contrived. I know I need to go deep and trust my subconscious to work out a way to weave all these loose threads together.

But I'm stuck; not with the first draft stage but with the very final stage. In my journaling, I discovered that I'm afraid I will not be enough, that I will put in the final massive effort and it still won't be good enough. I am holding back – I need to go really deep and I'm afraid if I reveal the most sensitive part of me, it still won't be enough – for my book and for me.

So even with this knowledge, I don't know how to progress. I'm feeling quite vulnerable here by sharing this. I hope you will have some suggestions for me.

ANSWER: I think of two things as I read what you've written. One of the reasons it feels so daunting, paralysing even, to get to work on your manuscript may be that you think of it as one huge step from where you are right now. And not just in terms of the work that awaits you, but also in terms of the results you so dearly hope for. It sounds like you look at it all from where you stand now and you don't quite see that this work, too, consists of a thousand small steps. You're steeling yourself for the big jump, but the gap is so wide! Of course you're terrified.

Can you call your attention back a bit? You have concrete suggestions from your writing mentor, right? That's something to hold on to in order to get started, and getting started is all you need to worry about right now. One small step, and then another. Can you find a little trust in the process that has led you this far? Can you find a small enough first step that you'd be willing to take it?

The second thing is that it sounds like you're trying to bargain with the universe, trying to get some kind of guarantee that if you go ahead with this vulnerable work, you will land softly on the other side. (And by the way, your vulnerability here is BEAUTIFUL!)

"I need to go really deep and I'm afraid if I reveal the most sensitive part of me, it still won't be enough", you say. It may be that it won't be "good enough" for publication even after you've done all this work (meaning that it won't be accepted for publication, which is not always the same as your writing not being good enough). It may happen like that and you have no way of knowing in advance. But what if your only way forward at this point is doing it anyway?

I guess I'm asking you to make an important decision. If doing this work and facing these particular fears is your only way forward – not just with this book but with your creative life – are you willing to do it? No guarantees.

During particularly scary phases like the one you're in, you might need to make that decision ten times a day. Commit and re-commit. And then get back to work.

All my love and support to you on this tender part of your journey,

Anna

CHAPTER 5

Radical self-care

"Creation comes from an overflow, so you have to learn to intake, to imbibe, to nourish yourself and not be afraid of fullness. The fullness is like a tidal wave which then carries you, sweeps you into experience and into writing. Permit yourself to flow and overflow, allow for the rise in temperature, all the expansions and intensifications. Something is always born of excess."

ANAIS NIN

WHEN I TALK about self-care, I talk about meeting our needs. Not as an afterthought, not if there's time left, but tending to our needs first. Fuelling up first. Before we've earned it, before we've proven ourselves or crossed the goal line. For most women, in the reality of our day-to-day lives, this is seriously radical. To approach self-care not as a reward or a remedy, but as a prerequisite.

Prerequisite for what? Your health and wellbeing. Your sense of worth. Your ability to know and enjoy pleasure. And your creative work.

We have a million strategies for increasing productivity and getting more done, even in the face of exhaustion; but they rarely involve kindness, pleasure or even basic self-care. Instead we grab for discipline, time-management, boot camps and seven steps to get to where you want to go.

Self-care is not about quick fixes. In fact, this is not about productivity at all. My goodness, let's not settle for productivity when there's so much more to be had. What I'm suggesting is that we devote ourselves to something entirely different – the art of overflowing.

If we do; if we tend diligently to our needs and fill ourselves up so that the flow through our bodies, minds and souls remains strong; then our creative outpouring increases too. We won't have to strive to make it happen. It will flow strong because that's what happens when you create a flood. Things pour from you.

Maybe this filling up could even be considered our most important job as creatives. I think so.

Keeping it close to home

The most important kind of self-care is the kind that doesn't take you out of your life, and that doesn't require a lot of money, time or resources. It's the most important kind simply because it's the kind that will get done. Just as we don't want to compartmentalise creativity – to keep it outside and separate from the rest of our lives – we don't want to compartmentalise self-care either. It's not something aside from our everyday lives – it's the bedrock of our everyday lives. It's what makes it sustainable.

We trivialise the importance of this sustainability when we make self-care a matter of massages and "me-time". Looking at it as a luxury makes it easier to dismiss or postpone. It also makes it a matter of privilege. What if you can't afford to get a facial? What if you don't have access to a quiet space where you can meditate, or to healthy food, or even clean water? What does self-care look like then? When the earth beneath our feet is being ravaged, what kind of self-care will sustain us?

Self-care is not about pampering. It is about tending to actual needs. Collective needs, individual needs. Human needs.

You have needs, woman. We all do. They're real and

they're valid and our lives – including our creative work – depend on us to tend to them.

Things change when we learn to take care of ourselves properly. We change. The things we ask for change, how we ask for it changes, the boundaries we uphold change, how we do our work and our lives changes.

That's what's truly radical about self-care – the way it challenges and changes us. How it challenges the status quo. When women decide to tend unapologetically to their actual needs, it challenges gender roles, relationships, workplace dynamics, it challenges the way humans interact with the natural world. Assumptions and expectations are turned on their heads. Maps are re-written. Change ripples through bodies, families and societies and every time it happens, we create a little more space for us to move. A little more breathing room for us all.

Pleasure first

"Pleasure is what fuels our ability to create and generate."
REGENA THOMASHAUER

As creatives, the body is our tool, the vessel through which our art is expressed. If we don't feel safe inhabiting our bodies, we can't express ourselves fully. It's easy to see this when it comes to actors, for instance. Someone who can't utilise her voice won't be able to make herself heard from the stage. Someone who can't embody the character she's playing is not going to convince us. But this is true for every creative expression, even those that might not seem to involve the body.

You have needs, woman. We all do. They're real and they're valid and our lives – including our creative work – depend on us to tend to them.

For a long time I thought a sharp intellect, a diverse vocabulary and a bit of wit was enough to make a good writer. I wrote from my head. What I didn't realise was that it made my writing abstract. It was smooth and elegant enough, but it wasn't grounded in human experience, in my experience, in the things I knew to be true about life, and so it never really burnt.

If I want to write something that burns, my gut needs to be involved. I know that now. My breathing needs to be involved, my heart and my hips, the little hairs on the back of my neck. If someone else is going to feel my words in their bodies, my writing needs to come from my body. I need to get in there and write the stories of grit and gut, blood and bone. The human story. Creating like that will cost a lot more than simply learning how to string together elegant sentences. We need fuel to be able to sustain this kind of creation process, and the fuel needs to be as raw and real as our creations. I think Regena Thomashauer is right when she says pleasure is that fuel.

Pleasure may sound sweet enough but it comes with heavy baggage. In the Christian tradition a woman's pleasure has been demonised for millennia, and variations of this theme can be found in most religions. The blame for men's unacceptable or "sinful" behaviour has conveniently been placed outside of themselves, on the woman. She tempted me. Her sinful body is the root of all evil.

The female body and sexuality must be contained and controlled in order to safeguard the paternal lineage – to make sure a man's child is his own. This control is the foundation of a patriarchal society and it is still woven into the fabric of modern western society. We see it in the way a girl's behaviour and dress is still considered a valid excuse for men's demeaning and violent behaviour. How sexually-active young women are sluts while their male counterparts are studs. How rape is criminal on paper, but goes unpunished in an overwhelming majority of cases. How women's right to birth control and safe abortion is constantly under threat.

Our bodies are not fully our own.

This controlling, shaming and blaming have been internalised in the individual and collective female psyche. We learn to distrust and hide our bodies and our sexuality. A certain kind of sexiness is desired and accepted in a woman, but it has more to do with being objects of male desire than sexual beings in our own right. If we embrace pleasure on our own terms we expose ourselves to judgement and sometimes to danger. So we learn to keep ourselves on a tight leash, ignoring our natural impulses and repressing our energy. In the process, we're cut off from our most powerful source of pleasure.

This is not a theoretical problem. In order to have full access to our creative expression, we need to have full access to our bodies; they need to be safe for us to inhabit. Right now, they are not. Most women have experienced some level of sexual trauma in their lives. Statistics say one in three, but for every reported case there are legions of silent victims. I for one don't know a single woman who hasn't experienced it.

Even if you haven't been subject to actual sexual violence, you have still grown up in a world where women's bodies are objectified, commented on and criticised relentlessly, in media, in advertising, in the schoolyard, on the beach and in the streets. You have grown up in diet-culture, where the size and shape of your body determines your worth. You have grown up in a world where women are made invisible as they age and change. If you made it through all of this with the connection to your physical self intact you are one in a million. Most of us have been severely bruised, if not crippled.

Sensual and sexual energy is strong. Pleasure is powerful fuel, if used consciously, and we have been denied that fuel for far too long. Reclaiming it is crucial for us as creative beings. And reclaiming it might look like wildness, like dancing naked under the full moon, like throwing ourselves into unapologetic sexual explorations. But it might also look like taking tiny, gentle steps. Working to heal a hyperactive nervous system. Learning to recognise when shame is triggered and finding tools to deal with it. Practising being present as we eat, actually tasting the food in our mouth. Learning to notice the way the breeze feels on bare skin, the way water envelopes the whole body when swimming. Being able to enjoy a massage. Finding out who we are as sexual beings, alone with ourselves, beyond the idea of the sexy woman.

This is the deep work of the creative woman. It's the descent from the safe, abstract realms of the mind into the body again, into the belly and the pelvis and the genitals and the feet. We don't want to go there because it is where the hurt resides. In our bodies, we carry the individual and collective memories; we carry the shadows, the emotions, the self-hate, the intergenerational trauma, the scars, the bloody trails of misogynistic, patriarchal history.

The body is the keeper of all our stories. But it's also where our strength and power is. The body is "the seat of pleasure, purpose and direction", says Bessel van der Kolk, M.D. We need to stand firmly, feet on the ground, if we are to do our work in this world. We need to root down into our own fertile soil, claim our right to our own pleasure and speak with authority about our own experience. Speak the truth, even when it doesn't look like the truth we have been told.

How do we begin? What do you need in order to feel safe enough to move forward?

Creating a sense of safety

To find out, you need to check in. Re-connecting with the body is the first and most important step towards creating a sense of safety. We can call it grounding, meditation or simply checking in with yourself, and there are a million ways to do this. You've probably tried one or two already. Keep it simple. Whatever works is good. Sit down for five minutes and pay attention to your breathing, or repeat a mantra you like the sound of.

What matters is that it helps you drop into your body, connect to your senses and return to the present moment. You want to bring your attention back, over and over again, until your whole being is still and you feel deeply connected to yourself. In that quiet listening space inside, you can experience yourself as you are, without stories and judgement. This creates a sense of steadiness inside, a reliability. You can trust your own presence. And in that presence, you can hear your heart speak.

Do it regularly. Daily would be awesome but life will get in the way sometimes. That's ok. Just don't fall into the "I don't have time" thing again. This is not something that will add a silver lining to your work; it is the foundation of your work. So make it a priority.

This is especially important when you go into a new creative project or when you up your game in some way. Fear and resistance will intensify, and you need to meet it actively.

There's a story about Gandhi that I like. Gandhi's advisors told him they had a very busy day ahead, with twice as much to do as usual, so could he skip morning meditation and get to work? Gandhi replied that if they had twice as much work to do, they'd better meditate for twice as long.

He knew that when things get busy on the outside, you need to steady yourself on the inside or you will lose balance quickly. Losing balance will slow you down and you will be more likely to make mistakes and take wrong turns, so in the end you might actually get to where you need to go faster if you take the time to meditate. You will definitely get there more smoothly.

Move, sleep, flow, connect

Another way to create a sense of safety can be to move the body, if you're able to. Run, work out or dance. Anything that makes us breathe and shakes us down into the body again will help break the spell. Sometimes that's all we need to do. Once we've released the tension and landed safely in the present moment again, we're good to go.

We can take a nap. A tired brain is more likely to get triggered and fearful. (To be honest, I've never been able to take naps. But just laying down under a blanket, closing my eyes and resting for a while is helpful too. I think it's the kindness that does the trick.)

We can try free-writing. Find a notebook, set a timer on five or ten minutes and don't lift the pen from the paper until that time is up; don't stop writing even if you don't know what to write. The uninhibited flow of words will release what's stuck in you, and remind you that you've lived through this fear before and survived.

We can connect to other people. Connection is key for humans and it's a powerful antidote to fear. We find safety in the pack; it's in our DNA. This is true even for those of us with a history of developmental trauma, where we grew up in relationships that were actually harmful to us. We might have to work harder to learn what safe connection feels like, and if we have issues with boundaries, we likely need help to develop a strong sense of discernment about whom we choose to let into our lives. But we need connection just as much as everyone else.

I disregarded this need for so long, thinking the only way for me to stay safe was to do it alone. But I've had to relearn. Feeling deeply connected to yourself and comfortable with your own company is crucial for your wellbeing, but so is connection to others. We experience the deepest sense of safety when we feel a sense of belonging to a group.

Now I also know that we create better, more impactful work when we allow ourselves to be part of a community. The right kind of friends hold a safe space for us and help us remember who we are when we forget. We are inspired by each other, we build on each other's work, we support each other's growth. Sisterhood has saved me over and over again and brought so much joy and juice back into my creative life. The lone genius is a tempting but flawed story. The truth is, community wins over competition in the long run.

If you don't have that kind of friend available, if you haven't found your pack yet, reading about someone who did what you want to do can offer comfort and connection too. Find some foremother and let her story strengthen you.

No more striving

How we take care of ourselves has a lot to do with worthiness. Am I worthy of feeling safe? Am I worthy of having my needs met? Am I worthy of pleasure? From looking at how we live our lives, the answer is no for most women.

I'm a recovering overachiever. I was one of those people who secretly took pride in how long I could go without sleep and how many hours in a stretch I could work, and I pushed myself far beyond what felt pleasurable, not to mention what was sustainable and healthy. I don't think the word "pleasure" was even part of my language at that time.

When health issues forced me to begin changing this pattern, it felt like learning to walk all over again.

Even to pause and go to the bathroom when I needed took a lot of practice. I usually didn't; I waited, just wanting to finish that article before I went. It sounds silly but this behaviour runs through everything. Dismissing the signs of my body as if they were somehow not relevant. I've had to practise simply paying attention to and respecting these signals. The simplest things. When I need to pee, I go pee. When I feel tired it actually means I need to rest. My body is not being annoying or spoiled. It's simply trying to tell me something. The message is valid. Go rest.

I'd love to say that exhaustion taught me this lesson once and for all and now I never stress or push, but I don't think that's how it works. It takes time to unlearn and relearn. Maybe some of us will always need to be extra vigilant because for different reasons we have that tendency towards over-doing. These grooves in our brains run so deep; they might never be completely erased. I don't think recognising this is a failure. Knowing myself – both weakness and strength – helps me make better decisions.

I'm a recovering striver and my default mode is still doing more. Always more. If I leave it up to myself to decide from day to day if I'm going to make space for proper breaks or meditation, I'm likely to skip it. Willpower is not enough to change these patterns, not in the long run. I need habits. I need to make self-care a natural part of my days, so I don't even have to think about it.

For instance, I love dogs, the way they love and give and play, but one of the main reasons I have one is because it gets me outside. Every day, regardless of weather or mood, I need to walk the dog. I don't always want to, but it *always* helps me feel better.

I'm not saying get a dog. I'm saying find ways to help yourself do the right thing.

Striving is a state of mind

I want to add something important about striving here, because we often associate it with the kind of behaviour I describe above; the overworking, the long hours, the pushing. And maybe you can't relate to that. Maybe your issue is that you don't do enough. You're just busy procrastinating and secretly wishing you could be more like those busy, pushy people.

But striving is not just in the doing. It's a state of mind. It's *how* you do your work, or even think about your work.

It's the non-stop repetitive thoughts in your mind about how you should really get going, how you should have finished this already, and damn, why can't you just... It's the stress in your body when you're *not* doing what you think you should be doing. It's the fixation on productivity and achieve-

Striving is not just in the doing. It's a state of mind. It's *how* you do your work, or even think about your work.

ment, the belief that it's your key to a sense of worthiness and happiness. It's the inability to listen to yourself and trust what you hear.

There's striving in procrastinating and avoiding, sometimes even more so than in doing. So yes, this applies to you too.

I want you to be aware of this because otherwise you might bring this quality of striving even into your self-care practice, trying to excel in it, doing all the right things in order to get maximum benefits. We need to be mindful. Adding self-care to an already overfull plate is not going to be helpful. And what's right for someone else, or even for you at a different stage in your life, is not necessarily right for you at this time.

Striving is how we do just about everything in our society, from performing well in school to dieting to being the perfect mother to keeping up in the career race. If we want to find another way we need to go deep within, because very few things outside of ourselves will support that search.

Practise receiving

Women are often held – and hold themselves – to a standard of selfless giving, always putting everyone else first. We don't know how to ask for what we need, and even when we are given what we need, we find it so hard to simply receive it. It's that whole thing about worthiness again. Am I worthy of having my needs met? Who am I if I'm not the giver, if I don't keep others happy? Will I still have a place in the pack? Receiving the support and generosity of others makes us vulnerable. We feel safer and more comfortable being the ones who give.

For a creative being, this inability to receive is perilous. When we cannot receive support we actually block the flow. We can't just flow in one direction, always outwards. In the long term, life must be allowed to flow to us as well as from us, or we will sooner or later find ourselves drained. What would happen if you start including yourself in the beautiful circle of generosity and reciprocity that makes this earth spin? Maybe you would discover that effortlessness is not the same as absence of work, but the absence of striving. Like a tree, you grow and evolve but you don't struggle to do so.

"With time, your roots grow deep and your branches long. You lean a little less backward in fear and a little less forward in doubt, resting solidly where you are. When the wind blows, you bend. When it stops, you straighten. Your boughs provide shelter and shade. Your strength supports the sky. Sitting quietly, doing nothing, spring comes and the grass grows by itself."
KAREN MAEZEN MILLER

In the moment of receiving we let go of the struggle, we allow ourselves to be filled up and then we flow. I know you've experienced it. It's the part you love the most about your creative work. The flow, the effortlessness, those magical moments when everything comes into alignment.

We can spend more time in that state. We can cultivate it. We are still required to do our share of the work, hard work at times. But it will be inspired doing. Joyful and effortless at its core. Very different from the striving we've relied on for so long.

Go find it

One way we can cultivate a state of flow is by committing to staying inspired. Inspiration is pure fuel. You fill up on it the way you fill up on food and sleep. It's part of a creative self-care routine and it is an excellent way to practise receiving.

There are plenty of misconceptions about inspiration out there, the most persistent one being that it's not in our hands. That we need to wait until it strikes before we can write, paint or dance. If this were the case, very little creative work would ever get done. You don't wait around for it to find you; you go out and find it.

Don't be too grown-up and sensible about it. The search for inspiration should never become some holy, solemn quest. You can find inspiration anywhere, in things completely un-related to your work, and you won't know in advance what will inspire you the most.

Go see a silly movie if that's what you feel like doing. Why not? The laughter might set something free in you and as a result you will express yourself more fully. Don't think it through. Don't be strategic. Just let yourself have it. You need this fuel and you find it by following the nudges of curiosity and joy.

The cyclic nature of creativity

We live in a culture of non-stop productivity and we have, individually and collectively, lost touch with one of the most basic facts of life – it's cyclic. All of it is. Night turns into day, summer turns into winter, gestation leads to birth, ebb is followed by flow. The female body itself is cyclic, our men-struation waxing and waning with the moon.

The creative process is no different. There are phases of intense growth and visible change, followed by periods when nothing seems to happen at all.

These quiet gestation phases usually unnerve us. This is when the pushing and striving sets in, trying to force ourselves into action mode again. We want consistent productivity, visible results at every stage of the process, or we lose faith.

What we're actually doing here is adapting to the ideals of the industrial revolution. It's important to be aware of this. When something feels like a universal truth, it's helpful to recognise that it's actually a construct; in this case a way of thinking that grew from the pursuit of economic growth.

Before industrialisation, we relied mostly on daylight to do our work; when night fell, so did our productivity. As most people lived in agrarian communities, the summer was naturally more labour-intense than the winter. When industrialism swept in, by the late 19th century, this changed. Electric light kept the natural dark of night at bay and shift workers could keep productivity up around the clock, all year long. No more adjusting to the seasons. Enter the linear world view. Human beings were asked, sometimes forced to adapt to the capacity of machines rather than the other way around.

It sure changed our world. Women entered the workforce on a whole new scale and the injustices and hardships they faced there gave rise to the fight for women's votes. The financial reality of nations changed and lifted so many out of poverty and into a growing middle class. But we lost something along the way. Something important. Because humans are not machines. We are soft, cyclical beings, and we hurt ourselves and fuck up our creative processes when we try to behave like machines.

If we try to maintain a constant level of productivity, we miss out on both rest and growth. When the slow phase is over and we are supposed to transition into the active phase again, we're depleted and weary from the struggle. We haven't rested. We haven't gone deep to find nourishment so we're too exhausted to make full use of the powerful active phase.

Eventually we lose the intuitive sense of when it's time for each of these phases. We can no longer distinguish between the natural call for rest and incubation and good old resistance trying to make us abandon our work.

And so it continues. Out of cycle, out of sync, stuck in our belief that we have to push and strive or nothing will ever happen. No wonder so many of us give up along the way, or find ourselves exhausted and depleted. It's amazing that we manage to create at all!

It's mandatory

Here's the deal: you can get by without taking good care of yourself and without learning how to properly fuel your creative work. People spend their whole lives that way. And you can get by; you can even get things done. But if you want more than that, if you want to access your full creative power, if you want to experience flow on a regular basis, if you want to actually enjoy the creative process, then learning how to tend to your needs is mandatory.

Whether you're an overachiever, an avoider, a dabbler or a procrastinator, it will be a stretch for you to let go of the fixation with productivity – the productivity you're busy with, or the productivity you're busy avoiding. The idea of giving to yourself before you have made any progress, before you've earned it, and when you really have neither the time nor the money for it, will feel uncomfortable at first. It will feel wrong, even. A lifetime of conditioning will work against you in the beginning.

To start with, simply pay attention. Learn about your own needs, as you would learn about the needs of a child in your care. Then move one step at a time towards a kinder, more sustainable way of being. It will change your life and work like nothing else. It will light you up; and your light is contagious, my dear. Your striving is not. This will be of the utmost importance when it comes to sharing your work.

Q & A

HELPFUL QUESTIONS about self-care, from women who have participated in my courses and workshops over the years.

What is the difference between striving and perseverance?

QUESTION: I'm not sure what you mean by striving. I find myself doing busy-work – filling out forms, trolling the internet, checking emails (for responses from publishers and from writing contests), cleaning up, rearranging my books or files. Is that what you mean by striving? Filling up time with non-goal-oriented activities? Or is it something else?

I think I am pretty good at looking after myself – I ask for help when I need to, both at work and at home, I share household duties with my husband quite evenly. If I don't go to yoga or to the gym it's not because I don't have the time – it's just because I am too lazy or too upset or despondent to go. It's for the lack of discipline.

I wake up at 5 and try to write. In the past six weeks I succeeded maybe three times – sometimes I go back to sleep, sometimes I don't even get up, sometimes I waste the time playing games, sometimes I just give up. But I keep on setting the alarm for 5AM. Often all I get is just fragmented sleep, because I don't turn off my snooze button and it keeps on ringing and I keep on turning it off. But I don't get up.

I keep on trying to do this, because of "pushing through resistance" – the mantra of creatives everywhere, as per Mr Pressfield. But I am not getting anything done.

So? Is this striving? Or is this perseverance?

ANSWER: You need to push through resistance, you say, like so many others (bless Mr Pressfield); but from what I hear it's not working. What you're doing is not working. You don't get out of bed, you don't write. So how about we consider this situation from another angle?

The most important aspect of self-care is what's going on

inside. How do we speak to ourselves? Do we give ourselves the recognition we deserve, even if we don't get it from outside? Do we know how to nourish ourselves deeply? Are we clear on what matters the most and do we make decisions and choices accordingly?

You call yourself lazy and lacking in character; this suggests to me that you are hard on yourself. Your inner critic is strong, and this is connected to a strong desire for outside recognition. Until you get it, you can't quite give yourself a break. *This is striving.* The relentless pursuit of a future goal, forsaking joy, health and self-love until we get there. Which, by the way, we never do. The goal line is ever receding.

Even though you're not actually working on your writing right now, you're still striving in your mind. Striving to start again, striving to get it together, striving to get out of bed, striving to get published and so on. Do you see what I mean? When I read your words, I sense a deep tiredness. Some part of you has had it with this striving and she's rebelling against every attempt you make right now. In order to break the deadlock, you need to listen to this part of you.

I'd start there. I'd take the pressure off from writing and moving "forward" right now. Decide that you're not going to write for two weeks, or a month. At all. Just give yourself a break – a real one. All those things you strive for, that you think will make you happy, give them up for a moment, and see what feelings and urges are hiding beneath the striving. This is deep water. This is where true change happens.

I know you just want to get through it quickly, so you can get back to writing. I know. But could it be that this IS your path back to writing? Could it be worth a try?

Love,

Anna

Am I allowed to choose what I want?

QUESTION: All this talk about self-care and pleasure as fuel has got me thinking. I think I've got it all kinds of wrong, for a long time. So much striving and trying, without really getting anywhere. Or, rather, getting everywhere. But without focus or flow.

I really don't know whether to try harder or go take a break. My intuition is lost! How do I get to a place where my intuition works? How do I break the habit of striving? Am I allowed to skip the news?

ANSWER: "Am I allowed to skip the news?" Substitute "the news" with anything you do that comes out of obligation or fear of missing out. If you struggle with overwhelm, this is a more important question than it might seem. You say your intuition is lost; but it's right there in this question, trying to bring your attention to something.

The question I hear you really asking is "Am I allowed to prioritise what I really want?" Spend some time answering this question; it will show you the way.

Go gently,

Anna

So stressed I can't even rest

QUESTION: As I've gotten older and learned more about energy & natural cycles it has transformed my outlook on self-care. However, if I become stressed or overwhelmed with work, self-care becomes the last thing on my mind. Part of this is because I will work harder to try to catch up. I also can't bear feeling like someone has unmet expectations or that I'm obligated to anyone, so I work hard to do what needs to be done. In the past this has looked like staying up through the night to make a deadline, or being on call 24/7 for support and emails, etc.

One of the issues I have now is that my plate is so full that even when I try to go to bed for rest & replenishment, my mind is so active with what needs to be done, and how so many deadlines are looming, and what I need to do the next day, that I don't sleep very well.

Today was one of those days that feel wasted. Wasted because it seemed that nothing went right, I made several irreparable messes, and wasted because I was so busy "striving" that 1) I did not get any significant work done, and 2) I did not rest, either. So I was neither nourished nor accomplished today. Grateful for input.

ANSWER: There's this strong sense of urgency about the work situation you describe, like you're running around putting out fires, out of breath and out of touch. It sounds like you wind up in your head at times like these. Making sure you're grounded is probably the one thing that would help you the most.

What often happens when we feel stressed and over-whelmed is that we try to up our productivity. We desper-ately want to cross some stuff off our to-do lists in order to feel calmer and more in control again. Our go-to remedy for overwhelm becomes doing more, faster. And as you describe, this doesn't work. The more you push, the less you get done, and eventually you can't even get rest "done" either.

What I've learned is that overwhelm ALWAYS requires a step back. Like fear, it's a signal to pause and take stock. In fact, overwhelm is fear. Stress is fear. It's the mind and body response to a perceived threat. This fear needs to be recognised and named, in order for your brain and body to calm down and function well again.

When you're stressed you don't function well. You can't make the distinction between what's important and what's not. You really can't; stress inhibits the executive functions of your brain. This is a big deal, because executive functions allow you to manage time, pay attention, switch focus, remember details, plan and organise, among other things. Without it, you run around as if everything is equally important and must get done NOW. And that's never the case.

If you have too much on your plate, then something will have to go. Too much is too much and no time management will change that. But even in order to see that, you need to step back and calm down first.

So in short – don't medicate your overwhelm with productivity. Pause, take stock, and then carry on accordingly

Love,

Anna

Complete and utter overwhelm

QUESTION: I'm not having a very good week – or month – for self-care, radical or not. I have an editing deadline for work, and a self-imposed deadline for NaNoWriMo – writing 50,000 words in November. I'm on track for finishing my novel but I'm behind for my paid editing job. It's also nearly Christmas, with a handful of family birthdays thrown into the mix. I've stopped meditating and walking, because there doesn't seem to be enough time. And I am so tired.

And when I read over that paragraph, I am appalled with myself. It's so "busy", so "woe is me." It's the opposite to

flow and it's not how I want to live my life. I'm really proud
of myself for writing my book so intensely and intently
but there is a price. I had a day in bed with a migraine last
weekend – something that hasn't happened for almost twelve
months. Hello – wake-up body call! What do I do?

ANSWER: I understand your frustration. You see this pattern play out but you're not yet able to change it. You're in
that "between" state where you've seen through it all, you've
had the insights, but your old patterns of behaviour have
the gathered momentum of a lifetime. They're still stronger
than your resolve to change.

I will gently ask you not to be too hard on yourself. It
takes time to change old patterns, and right now you have
enough on your plate without the added pressure of not
doing the self-care thing right.

See if you can start over. You stopped meditating and
walking, you say. Can you start again? What tiny step can
you take right now that would be kind and helpful? What
could you do to get a little more rest?

It's amazing what you've accomplished during the
writing challenge. Your drive is so strong. But if it's hurting
you, if your body is beginning to pay for it, then I'd give
that self-imposed deadline up in a heartbeat. I'd drop it like
a hot potato, mid-sentence. Just like that. Not because it's
not important, but because it's not *that* important. Nothing
is worth sacrificing your health and peace of mind for, and
your creative work really does not require you to.

This writing challenge (NaNoWriMo) is there to hold
and support you. If it doesn't feel supportive, I'd shift into
some structure that allows you to breathe again. Writing a
novel in two months instead of one, for instance. Or pausing
the project until after Christmas. You're allowed to adjust

and change when life doesn't comply with your plans.

What if you trusted yourself to do this work, even without the pushing and striving? What would that look like?

You have so much on your plate this month. Acknowledging this is not complaining, it's just being realistic. When things pile up I find it helpful to strip everything down to bare essentials. What is the least amount of work I can put in at this point, in order to keep things running? What can be stripped away or left for later?

This goes for both work and family life. Be ruthless. Are your expectations realistic? Maybe you don't have to be the perfect parent, partner, host, editor AND writer right now? Maybe there's someone who can step in and take some of the work off your plate? Most women I know, including myself, find lowering their standards and asking for help incredibly difficult, but sometimes it's the only way out of the deadlock.

Allow yourself to do it differently. See what happens when you do, and also notice what happens when you don't. You're not failing at this, you're learning. Be as kind to yourself as you possibly can in the process.

Sending love, support and rest,
Anna

CHAPTER 6
Share your work

"When you learn, teach. When you get, give."
MAYA ANGELOU

YOU STARTED ON this journey because you love your work. It lights you up. When you do it whole-heartedly, the fears and messiness of being human fall away for a moment. Your mind quiets and you are left with the beautiful simplicity of the doing. Just the doing. And it satisfies your heart the way nothing else can.

So why share it? Why bother going through the vulnerable, time-consuming and bothersome process of finding an audience and perhaps building a business around your beloved work? We all have our reasons. Wanting to be seen and validated. To get paid. To be part of a community. Yes, all of it. But there's something else too.

The joy you feel when doing your work is a gift from life to you. Sharing that work is how you give back. The work that truly lights you up is also what touches other people the most. It is your best contribution and it is needed, whether you can see it or not. And that's why we have the impulse to share it. Because we do, right? You do. Sometimes we don't even want to admit it because we fear that the ambition will taint our art somehow, or because it feels embarrassing to assume that what we have to give could actually be wanted by someone else. Women are taught to play small, not to assume that we are brilliantly unique and that our work matters. But the impulse to share it is there nonetheless and it's a powerful one.

The joy you feel when doing your work is a gift from life to you. Sharing that work is how you give back.

I think deep down we know that our creativity is not just for us. The creative power flows through us and it's not meant to stop there. We need to keep the faucets open and allow the gift of creativity to circulate, so that it can touch other people. So it can grow beyond our own limited reach.

Love the empty space

We keep the creative flow going by giving it all away, over and over again. We create and let go. This does not mean we give it away without compensation, it just means we find a way to share it. We don't hide it, hoard it or hold it back. We allow it to flow forward, to circulate. We make use of the gift given to us – our creative talent – and we share the fruits of it.

> "Giving the first creation away makes the second one possible. Bestowal creates that empty space into which new energy may flow. The alternative is petrification, writer's block, 'the flow of life backed up'."
> LEWIS HYDE

The nature of creativity is cyclical. We create and let go, create and let go. Letting go leaves us with empty space, and out of that empty space, new energy and new ideas are born.

We usually avoid empty space, either by hanging on to what we already have or by grabbing for something new to fill the void prematurely. We rarely recognise the emptiness for what it is – the birthplace of potential. We mistake it for barrenness; we fear it means creativity has stopped flowing. So we hurry up and fill the space with something, because something feels safer than nothing. And in doing so we block the natural flow. We get in our own way.

The natural state of creative energy is to move, always to move. We need to learn to work with that natural movement, as well as to allow it to work for us.

When you share your work, you open the door for more to come through. And it runs both ways. Remember, giving and receiving are required in equal measures. You keep the circulation going and more will circle back to you. This is true co-creating. Another force adds its powers to yours – call it the Muse or Goddess – and it will serve you, the servant.

It doesn't mean everything will be easy. It doesn't mean money will pour your way or that you'll be successful in the traditional meaning (although you may), it just means that your well will never run dry. You'll have plenty to give and you'll be replenished by the giving.

Is it useful?

I'm convinced that a society without artists and creators wouldn't last long. Artists are sanitation workers. We compost the waste of human existence. We gather the left overs, the pain, the questions and the untold stories and turn it into something else, something new. We connect the dots. We are the keepers of our collective memory. Without artist we would lose our way. We would drown in our own dirt.

Creativity can be a form of activism. We can criticise by creating. Since women's voices and perspectives have been and still are under-represented, simply expressing our truths can disrupt the status quo, shift conversations and invite new ways of thinking and doing.

"When women speak truly they speak subversively
– they can't help it: if you're underneath, if you're
kept down, you break out, you subvert. We are
volcanoes. When we women offer our experience as
our truth, as human truth, all the maps change."

URSULA LE GUIN

Creativity is never just a vehicle for our opinions. It's not
just a tool for us to use. It's the other way around. When we
align with the creative powers *it* uses *us*. But it doesn't mean
creativity can't be useful. Your voice and expression can be
immensely useful, but we don't always get to decide in what
way. We don't always understand how, until long after, when
we look back with the wisdom of hindsight.

For your art to be useful it doesn't have to be political or
born of outrage. It can be that, and it can be plenty of other
things too. It can be gently prodding, or visionary, it can be
a remembering, it can ask important questions, it can start
fires or provide cooling balm. It can offer solace and laughter
for weary human hearts.

The very choice to focus time and energy on creative work
instead of all the things we're told to value higher – such as
status, money, looks and approval – matters. To choose to be
a creator and not just a consumer matters. To be a woman
and decide that your voice should be heard matters.

Claim our space

In the 1980s, teacher Gunilla Molloy performed an experiment in her classroom that at the time caught a lot of attention. She counted the number of questions she gave to boys

and girls respectively during class, and found that she gave a lot more to the boys. Without letting them know, she then went on to divide the questions so that boys and girls got half the questions each. The reactions from the students were immediate. First of all, the boys complained that she was giving all the questions to the girls all of a sudden. They took it upon themselves to count the questions during a lesson, in order to prove that Gunilla was being unfair. Even when they found that the questions were actually equally distributed, they still felt that they were wronged somehow, proving the point of another teacher, Clay Shirky, who said that "when you're accustomed to privilege, equality feels like oppression."

At that point the girls began to approach their teacher too, imploring her to go back to giving more questions to the boys, since the boys were so upset about it and it made the girls uncomfortable to take up "their" space.

Several studies have since confirmed what is now called the rule of two thirds.[13] During an average lesson, the teacher claims about two thirds of the talking time, the boys as a group claim two thirds of the time left, and the girls get to share the remaining time (one ninth of the total talking time).

What matters most about these findings is that when asked, most of the students believe that boys and girls share the talking time equally. And when a teacher intentionally gives the girls equal talking space, both boys and girls experience it as if the girls get much more than their fair share.

Because we are so used to boys and men having more space than us – in the news, in museums, in history books, in classrooms, in boardrooms, in sports, in churches and so on – we have all internalised it as normal. And when we as women claim more space, it feels threatening to those who are used to having this space for themselves, but also to us.

173

This is important to be aware of.

Even when we claim space that by all rights should be ours, it might feel like we're doing something wrong, like we're asking too much, like we're being unreasonable, selfish or even aggressive – and that feeling will often be confirmed by the feedback we get.

Women who share their work, speak out unapologetically, or simply don't conform to traditional ideas of what it means to be a woman, can face a whole range of nastiness, from condescending comments to censorship to actual threats of violence. Both men and women suffer online harassment and hate speech, but when women are targeted it is more often gender-based, meaning women are attacked simply for being women, with the purpose of putting them "back in their place". Women are more often the target of gender slurs, threats of sexual violence, online stalking and so on. This goes even more for women of colour who not only face misogyny but white supremacy as well.

Even if our creative work doesn't draw that kind of attention, this still affects us. We see what happens to women who speak up and we learn that public spaces aren't safe for women. It holds us back, consciously or subconsciously.

This is why it's so important to create safe spaces for our work. To cultivate a sense of permission and trust in ourselves as well as find support in our community. Especially at the beginning of our creative careers. That way we can stand firmer if and when we face backlash in the public arenas.

"Any woman who chooses to behave like a full human being should be warned that the armies of the status quo will treat her as something of a dirty joke ... She will need her sisterhood."

GLORIA STEINEM

But what I don't want us to forget in the face of on- and off-line nastiness, is that when we share our work, we also make ourselves available to all the love, support and appreciation that's waiting for us, that we won't know about until we dare show ourselves.

We can create safe spaces for our work, but even if we do we can never fully protect ourselves from the judgement of others. We can't have growth without discomfort, we can't have public success without the willingness to fail publicly, and we can't experience the blessing of being seen for who we truly are without accepting the risk of being judged for who we are.

The risks of NOT sharing your work

There are risks involved in sharing your work publicly. But there are risks involved in holding back too. Like the risk of not knowing who you truly are and what you are capable of in this one lifetime. If you have the impulse to create and share your work but keep holding back, that unleashed power inside will eventually become corrosive and start eating away at you.

You know how that feels. It's the jealousy you feel when watching someone else do what you would love to do. It's the bitterness that seeps in as the years pass and you don't get around to it. It's the doubt that undermines your belief in yourself as you give in to fear over and over again.

Those are some very real risks too.

Fitting in vs. belonging

We all long for a sense of belonging. That feeling of being home in the deepest sense of the word, feeling welcomed and accepted as we are, connected to our family and our community, without ever losing the connection to ourselves. We are pack creatures.

Fitting in is what we go for when we've lost our hope of belonging. Fitting in is painful. It is trying to mould ourselves into a different shape in order to be accepted.

As women we do this quite literally; we squeeze into clothes aimed to hold some part of our bodies in and fill other parts out; we diet to change our shape; and if that's not enough, we reshape our bodies and faces through surgery. We believe firmly, because it is hammered into our heads from an early age, that only a certain body type, certain facial features, a certain skin tone and hair is beautiful. And those of us not naturally graced with that particular shape and form will have to reshape ourselves.

Internally, we wrestle with the expectations and unwritten rules about what a "real" woman is like. This ideal will shift slightly depending on your cultural, social, racial, religious and financial background, but one overarching theme seems to be that a real woman is likeable. She aims to please.

Sharing your work requires you to give that up. You won't please everyone. Some people will find you lacking; others will find you to be too much. Simply showing up will provoke some people. Get back in your place, woman!

But being liked as a result of moulding ourselves into someone else's idea of acceptable is a poor substitute for true belonging. By trying to fit in we lose connection with our natural selves, our voice and our power; and it hurts, regardless of how much approval we win in the process.

By trying to fit in we lose connection with our natural selves, our voice and our power; and it hurts, regardless of how much approval we win in the process.

You find your way back to belonging by listening to your-self again, trusting what you hear and acting on it. When you do, your life will begin to shape itself into something that fits the person you truly are. You will begin to feel at home there, at peace with who you are and how your story is unfolding.

This will take work, but know that when you belong in your own life, what other people think of you will matter less. This is crucial knowledge for people-pleasers. Before trying to belong out there – focus on belonging to yourself. Give yourself permission to be who you actually are and live the life you need to live.

"Success is liking yourself, liking what you do and liking how you do it."

MAYA ANGELOU

By valuing what is true for you over the opinion of others, you remain firmly rooted in your own life, your own soil, which is and always will be the safest, most nourishing and creative place for you.

Give yourself permission

We are lucky enough to live in a time when we can share our work easily. Many of the traditional gatekeepers are gone; you no longer need a record deal to share your music, or a book deal to share your writing. You no longer need a gallery to showcase your art, or a hefty advertising budget in order to reach your audience (although – let's be honest – it still helps). The online world has opened new doors for us and we are free to make use of them.

But many of us are still waiting for someone else's permission. Pay attention to this waiting. What exactly are you waiting for? Whose approval? Are you waiting for the boys in the classroom to say that it's ok for you to take up space? Are you waiting for some authority to confirm that you're qualified?

What would make it ok to move forward even without that confirmation?

What if you called yourself an artist, even before anyone else gave you that title? If you called yourself a writer, a painter, a maker, a creator, even if you haven't sold anything, or been published or publicly acknowledged?

What would change in you? What would change in your work?

I'll give you a hint. When you own up to who you are, your work will change, your energy will change, and how you present yourself will change. And the world will respond accordingly.

There is no mystery to it. It's a simple matter of authority, credibility and quality. Once you get serious about your creative life, you will produce work that reflects this commitment.

You might still have a long way to go from where you are today. If you are an absolute beginner you need to be patient about the time it takes to establish yourself and your work in the public space. Having faith that it can be done is not the same as being naïve about how much work it actually involves. Just remember that no matter how far you have to go, it's still only a matter of one step at a time.

Appreciate what you've already got

When we have a goal, we tend to fix our attention on all the things we have yet to do to achieve it and all the things we want that we haven't yet attained. The money we haven't made, the readers we haven't reached, the likes we haven't gotten.

Even if we did not start this work in order to get money and approval, most of us will at one point or another find ourselves lost in the chase.

This is part of sharing our work. We're human; we want to be seen, we want to be appreciated. We don't want to fail, and definitely not publicly. So how do you find the courage to invite people to a poetry evening at your house, having no guarantees that anyone will show up? How do you share something honest and tender on social media, hoping to have your work seen and appreciated, when you might end up getting only four likes?

Yes, let's go there. Four likes. You try to shake it off but the disappointment and shame spreads through your veins like poison.

This is a tough one. Look again at those four likes, and recognise that there are four people behind those clicks. Four actual human beings, who have each given you a moment of their attention and appreciation. Four people who responded to your work, who wouldn't have seen it had you not shared it.

If we cannot acknowledge the beauty and grace of being seen by these four people, we are not ready for – and will not be satisfied by – forty or four hundred either. We may think we will, and for a brief moment we might. But without awareness, the hungry ghost will be back, the need for more, always more, will push us to overlook and diminish the holy gift of those four hundred. Because now we want four thousand. It will never be enough.

Being disciplined about your gratitude will deepen your ability to receive. Sharing your work is about giving, but just as important is the ability to receive what is given to you in return, in whatever shape or form it comes. Receiving happens in the recognition of what you have before you. Four likes. Thank you.

The annoying beauty of it is that when you to let go of the attachment to more and begin appreciating and receiving what you've already got – one person, one reader, one client, one dollar a time – more of everything begins to find its way into your life. Profound gratitude is the holiest and most powerful of invitations, and it rarely goes unanswered.

True connection

Even if you want to build a business, you don't need everyone to like you. You don't need a million followers. You no longer need mainstream appeal, the way you did when TV and newspapers ruled. You can be as nerdy as you want; it will help people who are equally nerdy to connect with you. The more specific you allow yourself to be, the easier it is for your true supporters to find you.

Being specific means owning who you are, what you like and the particular flavour of your work. It means reaching inside for material, mining your life, your loves and your tastes, using what you find there to weave your stories and do your work.

This can be difficult for women because we're consistently told and shown that our lives are less interesting than men's. The stuff of our lives makes for women's literature, whereas the stories of men's lives make for literature. The male perspective is the rule; the female perspective is the exception.

When you share your work anyway, you challenge that assumption. You insist that your story and your perspective is valid and relevant.

You don't need more qualifications. You don't need to adjust and improve. You are good to go, just as you are right now. Your perspective is needed, just as it is. If you trusted this to be true, what would change about how you share your work?

Keep it coming

Of course we'd prefer our work to look impeccable and professional from the get-go, even though we might not actually be professionals yet. But it's a relief to allow yourself to be an amateur, to just start where you are instead of trying to come off as more advanced and successful. And it's a gift both to yourself and those who see you. Women and girls are in desperate need of role models. We are starving to see women do their thing, messily and imperfectly. Make a habit of sharing your process, not just the finished result. Share your enthusiasm for what you do. Invite people in. Keep the energy moving.

This requires you to challenge your perfectionism; but that's a good thing. Author Edgar Allen Poe said in 1846 that "most writers – poets in especial – prefer having it understood that they compose by a species of fine frenzy – an ecstatic intuition – and would positively shudder at letting the public take a peep behind the scenes."

Of course! Behind the scenes things are messy, and not necessarily in the romantic, bohemian way. It's snotty kids, tears of exhaustion, doubts and insecurities. It's draft after draft, us not knowing what we're doing, sitting our asses down to work at our craft, without a hint of "ecstatic intuition" (although sometimes we get lucky). The Good Girl was taught to show only what is finished and perfect in order to get approval, good grades and admiration. But this is not high school. This is life, your creative life; and here, process matters as much as product. Let us see you. We want to relate, and we can't relate to perfection. Sacrifice admiration in the name of connection. Let it be playful (remember play?). And above all, keep doing it.

Q & A

HELPFUL QUESTIONS about sharing your work, from women who have participated in my courses and workshops over the years.

Why is it so difficult to share my success with others?

QUESTION: I have so much fear about celebrating the things I have created and finished, even if I am immensely proud of them. For example, in a few weeks my second novel will be released. Of course I am extremely proud and excited. But somehow also a bit ashamed of the success, of having it published.

I have always been very "good". Good in school, achieving a lot, and as a result I've had a lot of jealousy aimed at me. I always hated the feeling that someone is jealous of me – I always wanted them to be my friends instead and did everything I could to play down myself and my work to please the other person.

I want to change that. I want to be proud, to celebrate my work and to recognise, without false modesty, all the work I have put into this book and other things that I have created. But it is so difficult! What are your thoughts on this?

ANSWER: First of all, I'm so happy for you, for your books and your emerging life as a writer! What you describe as your fear of success, holding yourself back and playing small, is something I can relate to a lot, as a creative and as a woman.

You mention that you drew a lot of negative attention to yourself growing up for doing "too" well in school. It could just as well have been for being too pretty, popular or athletic – anything that would have made you stand out too much. As girls, we are taught to compete for popularity and the attention of boys. But if we compete too well (meaning, if we begin to take up the space reserved for the boys) it becomes a problem.

You seem to have dealt with it by belittling yourself and

your achievements in order to appear less threatening. If being successful means we lose our friendships and "like-ability", we're likely to sabotage ourselves, or at least hold ourselves back from shining too brightly, just as you did.

Culturally – globally – this is a tragedy, but it kind of sucks on an individual level as well. You've done some awesome work; you should celebrate and we should all celebrate with you!

Allowing ourselves to celebrate our wins is a way for us to catch up with where we actually are in our lives and our work. Instead of just powering through to the next goal, we get to stop and notice that – WOW, I've actually made this dream come true! I started back there, and now I'm here! Look at the distance I've travelled! That feeling is powerful fuel.

Celebrating our wins helps us build faith in ourselves, and – this is important – it gives others permission to celebrate theirs too. But it can feel uncomfortable to be too vocal about our success. It can trigger a lot and we need to recognise this vulnerability as well. What do you need to feel safe enough to do it anyway?

Equally important is how we celebrate other women. Are we lifting each other up, raising our glasses and rooting for one another? I believe doing so helps us celebrate ourselves as well. It's a way to affirm that we're no longer competing and it will help create the safety we need to step forward.

Celebrating your light,
Anna

Who do I think I am?

QUESTION: This morning I woke up with a picture inside: My hands holding a bunch of feathers. I knew that the feathers were my creative dream; and they were so beautiful, so delicate and flimsy.

My first thought was gratitude. Here am I, with my dream in my hands, proudly holding things I have been blessed with and things that I have achieved myself. I've finished my education and I can go ahead and start sharing my creative work, my dream since forever. But suddenly I was struck by a massive fear – what if I lose them? A puff of air and the beautiful feathers are gone. A careless movement and they are gone.

Fear is always telling me I'm not good enough. And this morning all my fears seemed to have ganged up on me.

"Who are you to fuss about your precious dream, when others have to work just to make ends meet?" they roared. "Who needs your shitty drawings? It's ridiculous, why don't you call yourself an artist while you are at it?"

I held my breath and didn't move. I connected with my body and let all the fears flow through me, down into the Earth, just as you've taught me. I felt the need to push forward and go do something else to escape the discomfort, but I stayed with it and allowed myself to do a drawing of my hands with the feathers instead.

And now? What do I do? I so deeply want to hold those feathers in my hands…

ANSWER: What I hear your fear saying is "Who are you to do this work?" Right? If you remove the venom and the sharp edges from that question, it's an interesting one to respond to. Indeed, who are you to want this? Who are you?

Let's state it out loud here, because you are still hiding a little bit, aren't you? You're still afraid to claim the true scope of your dreams, especially in public.

You are the artist. You are the woman who is ready to do the work. You are the creative who is finding her way back to her rightful place in the scheme of things – as a co-creator.

Yes?

Some part of you is terrified of becoming visible, for reasons only you know about, but what you're telling me is that you're learning to hold this frightened part of yourself. This is key. You don't shrink away from the fear; you stay and deal with it as best you can. You let it flow through you instead of becoming stuck; and when you do that, creativity flows too. Your fears turned into a beautiful drawing!

As for the feathers being swept away and lost, well, maybe they will be or maybe they won't. What I hear is that you're holding them right now. Relax your grip, my dear. Enjoy their shimmering presence. Nothing else to do.

Love,
Anna

If we can't be ourselves in our work, then what are we even doing?

QUESTION: I haven't felt at home on my blog lately and I just realised why – because I haven't created it with myself in mind. I've been trying, and failing, to make my blog about "you" and not about "me", as all the business advice out there tells me to do. But this isn't a business blog. It's a blog about my personal journey, and the stories of the creative people I meet on my way, so I think I should be allowed to keep it personal. If it inspires others, that's just a bonus.

I had a plan to post an interview each week and a "journal" post each week on my blog. I had a list of dates and possible topics, and I felt excited about it at first. Then overwhelmed. Then I didn't want to write at all. And now I realise why. It's too strict, too technical. I'm not doing it for me.

While I commit to show up regularly for my own creativity by writing every day, I will not decide what to write about or when to post something on my blog. At least not yet, because then I'll just get stuck in my belief that it needs to be a certain way, or have a certain structure. It doesn't. It's just my blog. MY blog. I can post whenever and whatever I like. Journal entries, stories, interviews, poems, photography. This should be obvious but I didn't realise it until now.

If I can't be who I really am in my work, then what am I even doing, right? I want to do this for myself from now on.

ANSWER: I love what you're discovering about the connection between doing it for yourself and joy. This is what we lose when we allow our focus and our motivation to drift towards all the "shoulds". We lose the simple joy of creating.

It can be so confusing trying to make sense of all the advice out there on how to write for your business and so on. Some advice is useful, but it's good to remember that much of it is just accounts of what has worked for other people, at some time in their lives and work. It may not work for us, and it will not work for us if it means we abandon the soul and joy of our work.

So yes, allow yourself to keep it personal for as long as you need to. I wouldn't be surprised if this helps you create stuff that speaks to other people as well. Your journey home to yourself is usually the journey towards your true work.

And I also love that you're discovering what the struc-

tures that fit you and your work look like. You're right;
there's no rule that says you must post once a week. You
make the rules. The function of structure is to hold and
support you and your work, not to dictate the when and how
of everything.

Here's to the power of joy,
Anna

What does the balance between connecting and promoting look like?

QUESTION: I'm a writer, and as much as I love to promote
myself, I find myself enjoying content that isn't promotional.
This is such an interesting juncture for me; do I just engage
with my audience and hope they will consume my offerings
because they love me? Or do I actively market myself to my
audience? Of course we have to use our various forums to
promote, at least sometimes. We need to spread the word
about our work. But what does the perfect balance look like
for me? I don't know.

As time goes on, if I want to grow, how intentional (that
sounds better than aggressive, ha!) do I have to be in my
communication? Danielle LaPorte said that "wearing your
heart on your sleeve is great marketing." I get this, I do.
And yet I want to wear my heart on my sleeve because I'm
the kind of artist who wears her heart on her sleeve. And if
anyone happens to resonate, great! If not, I don't want to
push it. I want to trust deeply.

I also think it's important to allow oneself to feel inspired. If sending a newsletter twice a month is too much,
why not simply do once a month? We are now in an era
of digital overload, and less is truly more. Things that are

sent to me once a week seem constant and I can't keep up. Sometimes I long for the days where receiving an email was so novel and exciting!

ANSWER: I couldn't agree more with this. "If two times a month is too much, just do once a month. We are now in an era of digital overload, and less is truly more."

It's challenging to move in the direction of less when it seems everything around us is moving towards more. But still. Space. It's so rare these days to find the quality of space in someone's work, and when we do it's a long soft exhale.

There's much to say about marketing vs. just "showing up and allowing people to decide for themselves", and if we choose to turn our creativity into a business it is something we have to figure out. I like to think of marketing as the art of letting people know. If I don't talk about what I'm up to, how is anyone supposed to know? Really. Can it be as simple as that?

If we're in business, some aspect of our work needs to be transactional. It's just a fact. We need to put ourselves on the receiving end too or our business venture will be short-lived.

I can't stand over-aggressive marketing, but I do want to know what's going on for the people and businesses I'm interested in, and often I need a reminder too. So that's how I try to communicate myself. I tell my people what's happening, and then I remind them every once in a while – because we forget!

In the end, I think this worrying is mostly unnecessary. Very few creatives I know are likely to overwhelm their audiences with hard selling. Most of us end up at the other end of the scale – we don't even let people know, for fear of being too pushy!

Love,
Anna

CHAPTER 7

Creativity and money

"Money carries our intention. If we use it with integrity, it carries integrity forward. Take responsibility for the way your money moves in the world."
LYNNE TWIST

IF WE ARE to talk about the role of money in the creative life, I want us to get really down to earth and practical. I don't think we do that enough. I think we often allow ourselves to remain childish in our relationship to money, in a way that keeps us stuck and powerless. We dream of being discovered. We dream of swift breakthroughs, of all-powerful affirmations and mantras that will save us the actual work; we even dream of rich husbands. And we blame money, or the lack thereof, for all sorts of trouble. We curse money and we crave money and we remain ignorant about the ways we could work *with* money, if we would just go through the trouble to learn.

Some of this childishness can be blamed on the idea that we don't need to handle money as creatives. Shouldn't, even. The archetype of the starving artist remains strong in our collective psyche, and the beliefs and values we have attached to money are contradictory and leave us feeling incredibly conflicted.

On the one hand, money is irrelevant, we say. The best things in life are free and we're certainly not in it for the money (screw capitalism!). On the other hand, we dream about being recognised and making enough money to allow us to pursue our art without having to keep the day job.

So we crave it, and we disregard it. We desperately and

secretly want it, but claim it's not important. We judge ourselves and others for caring about money, and at the same time long to find a way to make our work profitable.

Ultimately, the starving artist represents the dream of stepping outside our everyday life. It's the dream of being excused, leaving the money worries and the diapers to whomever is willing to deal with it, because a true Artist focusses on art no matter what.

Which might work for you if you're twenty and still living at your parent's house – or if you have a wife at home filling in for you. If you don't, the starving artist is not going to be a viable path. You need a grown-up relationship to money.

Money is fuel

Accepting that we need to relate to money is a good start. Learning how to relate to it responsibly is the next step.

Many of us have learned that money is a zero-sum game. If we get more, someone else gets less. As long as we believe that, we're not going to want more money in our lives. Or rather, we'll still want more, but we'll feel ashamed about it and won't allow ourselves to receive it. Because we have good, generous hearts, we don't want to grow rich at the expense of someone else.

The truth is that money begets money, and not just in the sense that money invested in the stock market might grow. When we have money, we can hire people, pay for services, pay for editors, creators, healers, accountants and assistants. We can support artists and makers (including ourselves). We can buy good food and high-quality goods that don't strain the earth's resources. And so on. We create conscious wealth with our money and it is shared and multiplied.

It's a fertiliser. We use it right and good things grow from it. But how do we use it right?

I've spent an inordinate amount of time reading books about creating an abundance mindset, about magnetising and attracting money, about everything that's wrong with my thinking. Plenty of good points in those books. It matters where we come from, what we've been taught, it matters what we think and feel and believe about money.

But that's one side of it. The other has to do with practical skills, how we DO money.

If you're struggling to make it from pay cheque to pay cheque; if you're in debt, constantly overspending; if you have no clue how to handle the money you have; if you dread tax time; if your head is in the clouds or in the sand, no affirmation in the world is going to save you. You'll need to do things differently to get different results.

I think we prefer just working on our mindset, because we hope we won't have to take action until the discomfort is gone. We need to shift our mindsets, yes; but it's not until you actually DO it, until you face the friction and the discomfort of changing an old behavioural pattern and find ways to do things differently, that you truly ingest this new learning.

By doing things differently, you gather evidence for yourself; your lived experience proves to you it can be done, and lived experience always trumps theories. We need to start doing right away, even as we tend to the fears and the old beliefs stuck in our heads. The doing will bring about change, internal and external change. We need both.

And the first thing to do is to look at the way money flows in your life right now. Look at your bank statement. Does what you buy and don't buy represent your deepest desires

If your head is in the clouds or in the sand, no affirmation in the world is going to save you. You'll need to do things differently to get different results.

and values? Do you consciously use money as a fertiliser, and direct it towards what you want to grow in your life, or does it just randomly spread and disappear into nothing every month? Do you make choices that actually sabotage your chances of devoting yourself to your creative work? Many of us do.

> "Don't tell me what you value. Show me your budget and I'll tell you what you value."
> JOE BIDEN

Looking at money as fuel helps us relate to it actively and consciously. There's no doubt money can be used to fuel violence, war, inequalities and environmental destruction. We see it wherever we turn. We can use it to fuel the beauty industry, the dieting industry or big pharma. Money is not inherently good or bad; it fuels whatever we spend it on. It's our choice. If we use it well, if we allow our day-to-day choices to reflect our true priorities and values, if we use our money to fuel our own creative work and that of others – it can be a powerful force for good.

Women will save the world

I used to work in the NGO world, where it is common knowledge that if you want a society to thrive, you enable the women. You give them access to education and labour markets, you offer them loans and resources along with the right to handle their own money, and they will build things; they will make money and bring that money back to support and empower their families and communities in turn. This is now firmly supported by research.[14] The fate of nations is literally tied to the status of women.

This matters. If self-sufficient women act as agents of change in their societies, then it's important that women have money. It's important that women have not just symbolical power in the family and community but actual financial power.

Circumstances might be different for many of us who live in relatively wealthy western nations, but our relationship to money is still conflicted. We might make our own money, but we're not conditioned to actively relate to wealth the way men are. As girls, we are taught to be careful with money and to save it, whereas boys are taught to pursue money and to grow it, Sallie Krawcheck, financial advisor and Co-Founder of Ellevest, a digital investment platform for women, points out.[15]

And as adults, women's magazines assure us that the only aspect of money we need to worry about is how much those shoes cost. Instead of education about the underlying systemic money challenges women face – such as the wage gap, the debt gap, the funding gap, the domestic work gap, and the investing gap – we receive advice to clip coupons and refrain from buying that fancy latte if we want to improve our personal finances.

"This isn't about the lattes ... or any of the other ways we women are told we're deficient around money. It's about changing the narrative to recognize the real challenges we face as women and tackling real issues. It's about demanding a fairer playing field from our institutions (paid maternity leave, anyone?). It's about holding the companies at which we work accountable by demanding that they report out, and close, their gender pay gaps. It's about giving all of our children the tools to live the lives that they deserve. It's about balancing out our existing power structures."

SALLIE KRAWCHECK

We have masculinized money. Women are told in a thousand small ways that we're less able to understand and handle money. (Which is nonsense by the way; research tells us that, as much as finance is still a man's world, women actually out-perform men, both as individual investors and professional investors.[16]) We are still sold the dream of being rescued by the prince. It's a storyline that still runs through our culture. If you doubt it, take a moment to consider one of the most successful books of the last decade, *Fifty Shades of Grey* by E.L. James. The story of the young girl and the rich, controlling, handsome man pursuing her. See if it works to reverse the roles. See if it even works to remove his wealth from the equation. Nope. That's not a script we recognise.

Even in progressive Sweden, we need only look about a hundred years back and women were not allowed to inherit, to own property or handle our own finances. In the eyes of the law, we were not considered grown-ups in relationship to money.

Historically, none of the labour that has traditionally been carried out by women – the caretaking of children and old, the tending to home, family and community – has been compensated financially, or even been recognised as proper work. Now some of those roles have been professionalised, but even though the welfare of our societies depends upon this work to be done, it is still compensated poorly financially. The message has not been lost on us; women are supposed to give without receiving in return. Even now, demanding

The message has not been lost on us; women are supposed to give without receiving in return. Even now, demanding proper pay for our hard work brings shame to the surface, as if we're asking for something unreasonable.

proper pay for our hard work brings shame to the surface, as if we're asking for something unreasonable.

Getting into right relationship with money means acknowledging your right and your ability to act. No middle man (or any man at all, actually). No need for permission. When we do, we can begin to consciously fuel the things that truly matter, in our own lives and in society as a whole.

Three paths

When it comes to fuelling your own creative work, there are basically three ways to go.

One, you support your creativity. You keep a second job to pay the bills so that you can keep your creative space safe, sacred and completely outside of the demands of the market.

Two, you find a patron. The old way was to find – or be found by – a wealthy person who believed in you as an artist and wanted to support you financially while you focussed on your art. A wealthy parent or a generous trust fund would do as well. The modern version for those of us without an inheritance is applying for grants, or inviting your audience to support you through crowdfunding.

Three, you find ways to make money from your creativity. You choose the business path.

Many of us attempt a combination of the three. Sometimes we begin on one path but eventually find ourselves on another.

I'll say something about all three of these options, but mostly about the business path because that's where so many of us dream of going.

The second job

Choosing to support your creative work instead of the other way around doesn't mean you never share that work; just that you don't have to take market demand into account. You create on your own terms, in your own pace.

It's a peaceful path. Having your basic financial needs met creates a feeling of safety; it offers the freedom to explore and play without pressure, at a pace you can handle. It allows your creative work to be a thing of joy, something you turn to out of love.

Recognising your need for security (a roof over your head and food in the fridge) does not mean you play it safe in your creative work. It could be the other way around – because you don't have to worry about money or what other people are willing to pay for, you can go as wild as you like in your creative work. You can make all the mistakes you need in order to find your own creative expression and style, without having to shut down halfway because no one wanted to pay for your explorations. This kind of safety can be a breeding ground for true, bold work.

But you need to pay attention. With no external pressure at all, it's easier to get away with hiding and postponing. Never having a deadline might slow you down. All that freedom might make it difficult to focus and take action. This is why doing it publicly is important. You don't have to take market demand into account but you do need to create habits and structures that support you and your work. You need to get out there and find your community – people to hold you accountable. You need to honour the rhythm; create and let go, create and let go.

The patron

The sweetest of all dreams might be to have a patron. Just think of it – someone volunteering to pay you to do your thing. No need to keep a second job. No need to convince anyone or sell anything.

Of course, that's not the whole truth. Back in the days when those kinds of patronages were a thing, you still had to convince your potential patron of the brilliance of your work. This is even truer today, when the patrons available are not wealthy individuals but foundations, organisations and councils, and you apply for their grants in competition with thousands of other applicants. You do need to know how to sell your work; just not in the marketplace.

The newest version of this financial model is crowdfunding and content subscription services. This path overlaps the business path, since it requires a lot of work on visibility and regular giving back to those who have invested in you. In order for this to work, you need to convince people to support you. You need to deliver. And you need to know how to receive. This is not as easy as it sounds. Are you worthy of all that support? Who are you to even ask for it?

The crowdfunding alternative works best for those who already have a big following, so that all those one-dollar pledges add up to something substantial. If you're just starting out it's not going to generate enough cash to support you, but it could still be a piece in your financial puzzle. Even if you don't expect to make much money from it, it could be an arena in which you can share your work and it might grow over time.

In the interim, you either support your creative work with your pay cheques, or you try to build a profitable business around it.

The business path

If you want to make money from your creativity, you need to learn about business. You might not feel like it, but you need to nonetheless. If you want your creative work to generate cash for you, you need to know how to make it happen.

Get clear about what it means to begin with; what the costs and consequences are and if it's worth it or if you prefer to stick with supporting your creativity.

The consequences include having to spend time building and managing a business instead of giving it all to your creative work. It includes accepting how long it actually takes to gain stability and profitability. It includes having to learn how to sell (the horror!)

If you want to make money from your creativity, you need to be both creator and entrepreneur. And get this. The entrepreneur employs the creative.

This is where most creative small businesses go wrong. We'd much rather have the artist call the shots. We like it better when she decides what to spend our time, money and energy on. But if you go into business with the goal of making money from your creative work, the entrepreneur is the boss and her priorities will be slightly different from those of the artist. That's as it should be. She's looking after the health of your business, not just your artistic expression.

The embarrassing lover

So you decide to learn about business. When you do that, you also sign up to learn about yourself. You'll learn about how you avoid structure. How you're not comfortable with num-

If you want to make money from your creativity, you need to be both creator and entrepreneur. And get this. The entrepreneur employs the creative.

bers. How you find it so hard to receive. How you secretly think money is a bad thing.

You'll unearth a lot of shame.

The first time my business coach asked me how much money I wanted to make from a product I was about to create, I could not answer. First of all, I had no clear idea about how much I actually wanted to make. I hadn't done the math and didn't know what was reasonable. I kind of knew what I wished for, but I simply could not bring myself to say that number out loud. I was so afraid to come off as presumptuous and claim something out of my reach. I ended up saying a number so low that my coach said, "What? No, I mean in total, for the whole thing."

I was so embarrassed. For being clueless about money, for apparently not having an abundance mindset AND for even wanting money in the first place. Shame in every direction. Shame over asking for too much, and shame over not asking for enough. Hopeless.

It's like a bad love affair, one in which we're desperately drawn to but at the same time ashamed of our lover. That kind of relationship is not going to result in anything even resembling abundance.

Roots first, growth second

Building a business in order to sell your creative work is rarely a quick fix. It will take a while before your efforts begin to pay off, and it will claim a lot of time from your actual creative work. It's inevitable.

So when someone tries to sell you their recipe on how to make six figures in six months, know that what they're describing is the rare exception. Know also that they're probably not telling the whole story.

Trees, I believe, tell the whole story.

A tree always aims for balance between its root system and its crown. When planting a tree, the roots must establish before the crown can grow and flower, and the first season or two it might seem like nothing is growing. Nothing visible, at least.

This is applicable to financial growth as well. We must give ourselves reasonable time. A new line of work, a new project, a new business – they must all be allowed to establish and grow roots first, before they can yield a crop. "Why is it not taking off?" we say in despair after six months in business. Because building a strong foundation takes time. Because it's a skill in and of itself to make money, different from the work you already do as a creative. Because truthfully, you might not be ready for growth at this stage. Even though you think you are. Even though you crave it.

A few years back, I added a small line of art prints to my business. My second baby was three months old and the chronic inflammation in my back had flared up and hit an all-time high, which left me in severe pain with very little time and energy to deal with my business, much less a new venture. But I was so stressed out about by the fact that I wasn't contributing to our family finances that I went ahead anyway.

It didn't work out very well. The prints were pretty enough and I sold a bunch, but the growth I had hoped for simply didn't happen. I talked to a business mentor about it and she helped me see what I had been ignoring – that the current structure of my life and business could not sustain any kind of sudden or rapid growth. "What would happen", she asked, "if these prints took off?"

I had just a few hours here and there to do my work. I kept

all the prints at home and I had no system in place for mail or delivery. I packed everything myself, handwrote the labels, drove to the mail office and stood in line to get my stamps. It took forever just to deal with the few prints that I sold every week. What would happen if the orders started coming in by the hundreds, or even thousands?

The truth is, had those prints taken off at that time in my life it would have meant absolute chaos. I wouldn't have been able to handle it. I so wanted it to happen; I dreamt it would happen; but on some unconscious level I knew the truth and held back.

My business didn't have a solid root system at that time, and I had neither the time nor the energy to nourish it properly. Once I understood this I could get real about what needed to be done. First of all, I needed to accept the fact that my resources were currently very limited. Then, one small step after the other, I started the rather daunting but necessary task of rebuilding my work life and my business from the ground up – actually doing the work to create structure, healthy habits, financial systems, reasonable working hours and so on; not just keeping my fingers crossed and pressing "Launch". Yes, the prints had to go, for the time being anyway, so that I could give proper attention and nourishment to the right things.

When we have a structure in place that can support expansion, it feels safe for us to grow. When our businesses have solid roots, our lives won't be bowled over by success. Then we can earn money from our work, because we've created sustainable channels for income to flow through. But these things usually take time.

Roots first, growth second.

Stop fussing

Even with a solid root system, your business will still need continuous nourishment. We would never expect a plant to grow without water or enough light. But we often expect to harvest success and financial rewards without fuelling ourselves and our work properly.

It's a kind of magical thinking. We behave as if we're exempt from natural laws, mostly because we're trying to avoid the discomfort of receiving.

A tree won't fuss about its need for water and light. It won't say, "Oh no, I'm not worthy of receiving all of this, not before my flowers have even blossomed" or "If I receive this light and nourishment I'll be indebted to the sun and the rain forever." It just receives what is given, and therefore it grows. It's clean and uncomplicated. And incredibly effective.

What if we, too, could stop fussing for a bit? What if we could let go of our fixation with earning and deserving and simply allow ourselves to receive what we need? Wherever it comes from. If you support your own work, brilliant. If others support your work, brilliant. It says nothing about the true value of your work or the meaning it gives to you and others.

Which of these three paths, or which combination of them, you choose is entirely up to you. None of them is better than the others. Not making a dime on your creative work all your life is fine. Building an empire from your creative work is fine. What truly matters is that you keep doing your work.

Q & A

HELPFUL QUESTIONS about money and creativity, from women who have participated in my courses and workshops over the years.

What if I risk it all and lose my dream?

QUESTION: My creative fears are all about money. If I don't make money from my dream then I have to go back to doing some other work to get a pay cheque, or compromise as I have been doing for years. And then I might not be able to keep the creative spark alive. I feel as if I will lose my beautiful dream if I don't manage to make money from it. How do I dare take such a huge risk?

I wish sometimes that I was content with an ordinary life, with a "common" job, but I'm not and I know I must create my own reality.

ANSWER: Beneath the fear of not making money we usually find deeper fears. You mention one of them here – that you'd fail and be forced to go back to a day job you're not passionate about and eventually you'd lose the will and courage to try any more. You'd lose your dream. And that would be such a huge loss; you'd rather let it stay a dream.

But keeping the dream a dream in order to not to lose it is a poor substitute for actually living it. A dream, however beautiful, is just a dream. It's not real and it can't truly nourish you. Preferring the safe fantasy to real life keeps us securely stuck where we are.

What is really important for you to remember, and for anyone who has issues with money and safety to remember, is that it's ok to go slow. There's no need to make a big, dramatic leap into the unknown. If you do, you'll probably scare yourself into paralysis anyway. Taking one small step after another, making progress while also keeping your stress levels manageable, is a better option. And it's enough. It will get you where you want to go. But you need to start. You need to decide that it's worth the risk.

There's something you write that makes me think you haven't made that decision yet. You say that you wish you could be content with a "common" life, that you could be happy just working your day job and not have this longing for more.

But is that really true? Is that truly what you wish for?

What's the message beneath those words? That you'd rather be rid of the dream. That you haven't recognised the gifts and blessing of a creative calling but see it only as a burden. In order to co-create with your dream, you need to make the decision. Yes, I'm doing this (however slow), and yes, it's worth it; thank you for choosing me to walk this path. Once you do, once you commit and start acting on it, things can start to move and shift.

No rush. One step at a time in your own pace.

Love,

Anna

What if you do what you love and the money doesn't follow?

QUESTION: We often get this message: Do what you love and the money will follow. But I don't think that's the experience of many creative and passionate entrepreneurs. We do what we love and the money doesn't follow.

I know Elizabeth Gilbert, in her latest book, said that she promised her writing that she would support it. That it would never have to support her. And that's what allowed her writing to thrive. But I know many of us would love to make money doing what we love. If that's the case what is the disconnect? What are we missing to make that a reality? Or are we buying into a pipe dream and should we really

be following in Elizabeth Gilbert's footsteps without any promise of ending up with the success that she has?
Alishia

ANSWER: Right. If we just do what we love, the money will follow. You're not the only one who has dispaired reading those words. There's a bit more to it than that.

I think Elizabeth Gilbert chose a very peaceful path when she decided that she would not rely on her writing to support her financially. It removes so much pressure; and when it comes to creative work, you know that's a good thing. Things flow better when we're relaxed.

But if you really want to make a business out of your creative work, if you really do want it to support you – well then you have work to do. Not just your creative work; but also the work of learning about business, money management and money mindset.

Most of us skip that part. Wouldn't it be sweet if it all we needed to do were to follow our passion and repeat the right affirmations? But money is a complex subject. It's a relationship, it's mindset AND practical work. This is a good thing. It means we can learn more about it and begin to do it differently. And when we do it differently we will get different, better results.

Love,
Anna

Why do I feel so uncomfortable being supported by my husband while I write?

QUESTION: My husband and I aspire to live together as equals. We've always been mindful of who does what in our home, trying to make sure we don't fall into out-dated gender roles.

Our finances are joined and we contribute according to ability. For a time, I've been working a lot more than is comfortable, being both employed and working on my third book. Now my employment has ended unexpectedly, and my husband suggested that should I focus on writing for a while instead of finding a new job right away, and that he would cover our costs in the meanwhile. This is such a generous offer and it's what I want too: to finish my book before I take on new work. But I didn't expect it to feel quite so uncomfortable to receive his financial support. The feminist in me rebels. Here I am, financially dependent on a man – albeit temporarily; the very opposite of what I've been striving for my entire adult life.

The paradox is that I've been supporting him, contributing more to our mutual finances in the past, and I've been perfectly comfortable with that, but being in the receiving end turns out to be a lot more difficult. What do I do?

ANSWER: You do what works. For both of you, for your specific circumstances, for this time in your lives. It's not inherently wrong to be supported by your male partner – it's just that this arrangement comes with a lot of baggage. That baggage has to do with power dynamics. For you – as a feminist and as a woman – this arrangement brings up fears – and maybe also shame for willingly putting yourself in a situation that has been the trap of so many women, that maybe you have sworn to never fall into. To be financially independent is truly a key to freedom in so many ways. BUT. Your situation is different.

For the two of you, him supporting you does not mean that he's the head of the household, or that he has any claim on you beyond what you both have on each other for being in a committed relationship. It's a practical arrangement. It's a generous offer from him, coming from love, most likely. Just like you have supported him out of love in the past.

You can step into it with eyes wide open. You can talk to each other about your fears. You can set a time limit to help you trust that it really is temporary. And if you notice that it feels too stressful, or that it impacts your relationship in a negative way, you can change your mind about it. Find another way to do it.

It's complicated, because of the historical context, because we still live in a patriarchal society. If you have kids, it gets even more complicated. Let's not pretend otherwise. But also don't let that stop you from trying. See what happens, you can change your mind at any time.

Good luck!

Anna

Afterword

I BELIEVE IN the doing. I believe in using our hands and minds and hearts and voices to do our work. I believe in our commitment to this work; in the unlearning and re-learning of almost everything. One step at a time. This is a life's work.

There is so much that needs to change; politics and paradigms that need to shift, governments that need to fall, power structures that need to be dismantled. But we can't wait for that part of the work to be done before we start creating. We need to start right now, in the midst of the mess. We need to start before the world is ready, before WE are ready. We need to start.

We need to kindle our fires; not just barely keeping the embers alive, but feeding those fires to a roaring blaze of light and heat that will transmute everything, and we can light our torches off those fires, one after the other; and hold them high, illuminating the path for ourselves and each other.

When we start doing, we become changemakers. We become healers, weaving new stories, truer stories, reclaiming what is ours and rewriting the rules. Creating this world as it should be.

I know for sure that sisterhood will save us. We will do it together.

We will root down. We will reconnect. And we will keep doing our work.

Gratitude

For helping me create this book:
Åsa-Saga Hammarstedt – who helped me navigate the
crazyness of self-publishing and online marketing.
Lisa Zachrisson – who designed the book so beautifully.
Jonna Lovind – who helped me create the illustrations and
whose creativity is a constant source of amazement for me.
Michelle McCartan – who became my writing buddy, held
me accountable and reminded me I'm not alone.
Jeanette Encinias – who took care of my first draft and
helped me make it so much better.
Tamsin Kilner – who helped me get the grammar right.
Mats Lehnberg – who made my rumpled paintings digital.
Sadie Rose Casey – who generously answered all my ques-
tions when I first set out on this project.

For keeping me sane:
Eva Nylander – who is my sister, my sounding board and my
constant companion.
Mia Lehnberg and Karin Sveland Ludvigson – who have
offered me sisterhood and breathing room, read my work
and helped me articulate my ideas.
Charlotte Alfvin and Tatini Montgomerie – whose friendship is solid rock beneath my feet.
Ann Rosman – who told me to get my shit together and start

writing already, enough times for me to actually hear it.
Mom – who has been babysitting, cooking, cleaning and
supporting me in so many ways.
Farfar (my paternal grandfather) – who knew I'd be a writer
long before I knew it myself. I miss you. I wish you were here
to see my first book.
Isa Söderström – whose imagination always ignites mine.
Kristina Lander – my therapist, who helped me finally
understand and create safety in my life.

For endless inspiration:
My course participants – who asked brilliant questions and
helped me sharpen my answers.
Natashja Blomberg – who fanned the flames of my righteous
anger and helped me become a more unapologetic feminist.
Mia Skäringer – who inspired me to give less fucks about
what people think about my work.
Judith Maria Bradley – who proved to me that a woman's
power and brilliance only grows with age.
Rachel Cargle – who has taught me some necessary lessons.
Carrie-Anne Moss – who offered me space and showed me
how to lead.
Hiro Boga – who told me the truth and gave me the tools.
Marjorie Miller – whose paintings inspired mine.
Staffan Larsson – whose art will forever inspire me and who
allowed me to paint his dancer in my own style for the cover.

For everything:
Jens – who have walked alongside me, faced my obsessive
relationship to writing with equinimity, supported me
through the rough patches of entrepreneurship, and loved
me through all the doubts.
Elsa – my cannonball, my bundle of fire and love, who
challenges my ability to say no on the daily.

Endnotes

1 Weinberg & Kapelner. Comparing Gender Discrimination and Inequality in Indie and Traditional Publishing. *PLoS ONE*, 2018

2 Fredrickson & Roberts. Objectification theory: Toward Understanding Women's Lived Experiences and Mental Health Risks. *Psychology of Women Quarterly*, 1997

Fredrickson, Roberts, Noll, Quinn & Twenge. That Swimsuit Becomes You: Sex Differences in Self-objectification, Restrained Eating, and Math Performance. *Journal of Personality and Social Psychology*, 1998.

McKinley & Hyde. The Objectified Body Consciousness Scale – Development and Validation. *Psychology of Women Quarterly*, 1996.

3 Fredrickson & Roberts. Objectification Theory: Toward Understanding Women's Lived Experiences and Mental Health Risks. *Psychology of Women Quarterly*, 1997

4 Dunning & Ehrlinger. How Chronic Self-views Influence (and Potentially Mislead) Estimates of Performance. *Journal of Personality and Social Psychology*, 2003.

Institute of Leadership and Management. *Ambition and Gender at Work*. 2011.
Bleidorn, Davis, Arslan, Denissen, Rentfrow, Gebauer & Potter. Age and Gender Differences in Self-Esteem — A Cross-Cultural Window. *Journal of Personality and Social Psychology*, 2015.

5 Goldman Sachs Global Markets Institute. *Closing the gender gaps: Advancing women in corporate America*. 2018

Heidrick & Struggles. *Route to the Top* 2018.

6 Chavisa Woods. Hating Valerie Solanas (And Loving Violent Men). *Full Stop.* 2019.

7 Deloitte US. *Global Mobile Consumer Survey.* 2018.

8 Stothart, Mitchum & Yehnert. The Attentional Cost of Receiving a Cell Phone Notification. *Journal of Experimental Psychology: Human Perception and Performance*, 2015.

9 Ward, Duke, Gneezy & Bos. Brain Drain: The Mere Presence of One's Own Smartphone Reduces Available Cognitive Capacity. *University of Chicago Press Journals*, 2017.

10 The average lifespan of a Swedish woman is used in this example.

11 Statistics Sweden. *Mäns hushållsarbete ökar – men kvinnorna gör fortfarande mest hemma.* 2011.

12 Babcock, Recalde & Vesterlund. Why Women Volunteer for Tasks That Don't Lead to Promotions. *Harvard Business Review*, 2018.

13 Eliasson, Sørensen & Karlsson. Teacher–student interaction in contemporary science classrooms: is participation still a question of gender? *International Journal of Science Education*, 2016.

Eliasson. *Att kommunicera skolans naturvetenskap: ett genusperspektiv på elevers deltagande i gemensam och enskild kommunikation.* Mittuniversitetet, 2017.

14 Lopez-Claros & Nakhjavani. *Equality for Women, Prosperity for All – The Disastrous Global Crisis of Gender Inequality.* St Martin's Press, 2018.

15 Krawcheck. *Just buy the f***ing latte.* Fast Company, 2019.

16 Stewart. *Are women better investors than men?* Warwick Business School, 2018

Barber & Odean. Boys Will be Boys: Gender, Overconfidence and Common Stock Investment. *Quarterly Journal of Economics,* 2001

Resources

A Room of One's Own, by Virginia Woolf

All the Rage: Mothers, Fathers, and the Myth of Equal Partnership, by Darcy Lockman

Being and Being Bought: Prostitution, Surrogacy and the Split Self, by Kajsa Ekis Ekman

Beloved, by Toni Morrison

Big Magic, by Elizabeth Gilbert

Bird by Bird, by Anne Lamott

Burning Woman, by Lucy H. Pearce

Collected Essays, Prose, and Stories, by Alice Walker

Dancing at the Edge of the World: Thoughts on Words, Women, Places, by Ursula K. Le Guin

Does it Matter? Essays on Man's Relations to Materiality, by Alan Watts

100 Essays I Don't Have Time to Write, by Sarah Ruhl

Frida Kahlo: Face to Face, by Judy Chicago

Georgia O'Keeffe: A Life, by Roxana Robinson

Gift from the Sea, by Anne Morrow Lindbergh

Hateship, Friendship, Courtship, Loveship, Marriage, by Alice Munro

I Know Why the Caged Bird Sings, by Maya Angelou

Jag vill sätta världen i rörelse: En bigrafi över Selma Lagerlöf, by Anna-Karin Palm

Jane Austen, Obstinate Heart: A Biography, by Valerie Grosvenor Myer

Just Kids, by Patti Smith

Karin Larssons värld, by Lena Rydin

Kvinna i avantgardet: Sigrid Hjertén - liv och verk, by Görel Cavalli-Björkman

Long Life: Essays and other Writings, by Mary Oliver

Mary Magdalene Revealed: The First Apostle, Her Feminist Gospel & the Christianity We Haven't Tried Yet, by Meggan Watterson

Minor Characters, by Joyce Johnson

Momma Zen, by Karen Maezen Miller

Moon Moods, by Sadie Rose Casey

Outrageous Acts and Everyday Rebellions, by Gloria Steinem

Own It: The Power of Women at Work, by Sallie Krawcheck

Playing Big, by Tarah Mohr

Pussy: A Reclamation, by Regena Tomashauer

Sister Outsiders: Essays and Speeches, by Audre Lorde

Succulent Wild Woman, by Sark

The dance of the Dissident Daughter, by Sue Monk Kidd

The Artist's Way, by Julia Cameron

The Beauty Myth: How Images of Beauty are Used Against Women, by Naomi Wolf

The Bell Jar, by Sylvia Plath

The Body Keeps the Score, by Bessel van der Kolk

The Diary of Anais Nin, Volume 4, by Anais Nin

The Essential Rumi, translations by Coleman Barks

The Gift, by Lewis Hyde

The God of Small Things, by Arundhati Roy

The Handmaids Tale, by Margaret Atwood

The Red Shoes: Margaret Atwood Starting Out, by Rosemary Sullivan

The Soul of Money, by Lynne Twist

The Writing Life, by Annie Dillard

This is the Story of a Happy Marriage, by Ann Patchett

To Be Soul, Do Soul, by Hiro Boga

We Tell Ourselves Stories in Order to Live: Collected Nonfiction, by Joan Didion

Women Who Run with Wolves, by Clarissa Pinkola Estés

Writing Down the Bones, by Natalie Goldberg

ANNA LOVIND is a feminist writer who believes in women's creative freedom and the power of our voices and stories.

Anna left a career as an editor at a major publishing house, moved to the countryside and set out to build a business that supports her own and other women's pursuit of a meaningful and sustainable creative life.

Since then, she has coached bestselling authors, helped launch solo entrepreneurs into orbit, and guided creatives from all over the world to go from dreaming to doing through her courses and workshops. In 2016, she co-founded Write Your Self, a writing teacher training with a mission to spread knowledge about how to use writing as a tool for healing.

Anna lives in the deep forests of Dalarna, Sweden, with her man, their two kids and a dog.

Visit Anna's world on annalovind.com